Out of the Melting Pot

Out of the Melting Pot

Bob Gordon

Marshalls

Marshalls Paperbacks
Marshall Morgan & Scott
3 Beggarwood Lane, Basingstoke,
Hants, RG23 7LP, UK

ISBN 0 551 01164 5

Typeset by Alan Sutton Publishing Ltd, Gloucester
Printed in Great Britain by Anchor Brendon Ltd.,
Tiptree Colchester.

Contents

To Katie

'*The crucible for silver and the furnace for gold, but the Lord tests the heart*'

Proverbs 17.3

Acknowledgements

A book like this cannot be written without the help and fellowship of a great number of people. After all it is only one man's expression of what has taken place in the life of a whole fellowship. I am grateful to God for allowing me to experience faith within the context of the Bethany Fellowship. I am grateful to my fellow believers in the Fellowship for their understanding and trust as many of the challenges of faith have been worked through within my own life.

In particular I want to say thank you to Esther McCulloch who has given so much time and energy to the typing of the original manuscript and without whose help the book would never have been completed in time.

I have dedicated this book to my friend and personal assistant for the last five years, Katie Bacon. We have shared many of the struggles as well as the victories of faith for almost ten years. Words cannot express my indebtedness to her for her help in the ministry over these past few years and I pray that as she goes forward in her married life with Jeremy she will continue to know the power of faith in their life together.

Preface

To some people this might seem only to be a book about a remarkable story of how God provided six hundred thousand pounds within a short space of time to buy what is now Roffey Place Christian Training Centre. It is that. But it is much more than that. It is about faith.

I believe that faith is not only the fundamental principle of Christian experience it is the most important element for Christian living. The epistle to Hebrews tells us that without faith it is impossible to please God. For me one of the most directly challenging questions of the whole New Testament lies in the words of Luke 18.8:

> "However, when the Son of Man comes will he find faith on the earth?"

For many people today faith is a lost art. They have mislaid the key to the Kingdom. Others operate with a very naive view of faith. They equate faith with a kind of spiritual magic through which we can manipulate God to do just as we please. Faith is not like that. Faith is a many splendoured thing. It is a gift from God and is precious to the heart of God.

I have used the story of how God provided the money for Roffey Place as an interweave in the story of faith. My prayer is that you will not be left only with the impression of a miracle but with an insight into a miracle working God. I have tried to be honest not only about the miracles of faith but about the struggles of faith. For every empty tomb has its Gethsemane and I sometimes fear that today we want all the glory and none of the cost.

I ended my previous book *How Much More* by saying that faith has become the most exciting venture of my life. There is no other way to live as a Christian: it is the only way that God can fulfil his purpose through us and it is the only way we can enter into our full inheritance as sons and daughters of the Kingdom. When we learn to live by faith we will see the power of God released through our lives to a degree that we never imagined possible.

Little did I know then what lay immediately ahead. All I can say is that these subsequent experiences of God recorded in this took only confirm what a mighty God we have.

TO GOD BE THE GLORY GREAT THINGS HE HAS DONE!

Bob Gordon

I

Into the fire

Grahame Scofield passed the file over nonchalantly. In his usual easy going way he invited me to have a look at it. It was fantastic. The file contained the advertising blurb from a local estate agent about a large property nearby that was for sale. As I read the details my heart began to race because here, in front of my eyes, was the fulfilment of a dream that I had carried for almost ten years.

I had felt for a long time the need to be able to disciple men and women into the deeper ways of God through the work of the Holy Spirit – especially men and women who themselves were involved in ministry and leadership so that they could come to understand the principles of ministering in the power of the Holy Spirit today.

I had joined Colin Urquhart and the work of Bethany Fellowship about a year before this event and had discovered that Colin was living with the same kind of burden as I was. As I read through the file I saw clearly that Roffey Place was just the sort of place that was tailor-made for the vision.

For the past four years it had been the national training headquarters of the Royal Society for the Prevention of Cruelty to Animals. They had bought it and re-furbished it thoroughly to suit their needs but things hadn't worked out and it had been under-used and had become something of a white elephant to them. Now it was up for sale.

I read on through the file and, as I looked at some more details, I could see it functioning under the power and direction of God as a place where many men and women could learn faith and power in a family context in a first-hand way. I was excited. The complex was no more than nine years old and had been built at the side of a much older Queen Anne house which had itself been completely renovated. Everything was there: fully fitted classrooms which suited our needs right down to the ground, kitchen and dining facilities that were equipped with every necessity and which had hardly been used at all, and bedrooms with all the furniture and fittings and bedding in place ready for new occupants. Even the service plant was in great order: boilers, sewage plant, gardening equipment, audio-visual aids, offices, the lot. It was very good. There were total facilities to take about fifty students, plus houses and flats for staff. I could just see how it would all fit together. It was like a dream.

Then I turned the page and saw the price! They were asking for offers over six hundred thousand pounds. My heart sank. I looked at Grahame and he smiled a wry smile. That's his way. I took the brochure and put it in my desk drawer with some appropriately pious comment. Deep down in my heart I thought, 'It's too much'. If it had been three hundred thousand pounds or so it might have been better, but six hundred thousand!

What was more, I heard on the grapevine that other parties were interested and that they had cash available. I suppose I have to admit that deep down I did not really think it was possible. My reaction was probably governed by another factor anyway. In the last year or so as an Elder of the Bethany Fellowship I had been involved in some amazing movement of faith. We had set up a new resources centre at Balcombe for which the Lord had provided around a hundred thousand pounds. We had established the work of Abbots Leigh under the direction of David Brown. Abbots Leigh is a fifty acre farm with a large house in which a spiritual rehabilitation work has been founded amongst the poor and needy. Many people who have lived under the domination of drugs, drink, sex and brokenness have found power for a new life in Christ through that ministry. To add to that work we had then bought an old cinema in Brighton which has become a logical extension of the work in Abbots Leigh. It is used as an evangelistic outreach centre right in the front line of need. A transformation has taken place in what was a derelict cinema-turned-bingo-hall. No longer does the clickety-clack of bingo machines ring through the building: now it's the praise of Jesus as those released in Christ find something new to sing about. All of this had taken another three hundred and fifty thousand pounds or so, but here was I looking a six hundred thousand pound challenge in the face.

Something prevented me from discarding the brochure at that moment, but at the same time I did not feel we could go on. For the next three weeks it lay in my drawer until one day Colin Urquhart came to my study. I showed him the brochure. He looked at it and his reaction was much the same as mine – 'great but too expensive'.

The thought stayed in our minds until one morning I received a phone call from Paul, one of our lawyers. It was Tuesday and he told me that he had heard on the grapevine that the property at Roffey Place was to be sold to the highest bidder the following Friday. Bids were to be in the hands of the agents by nine o'clock that Friday. My heart quickened because in the intervening weeks I had not forgotten the property but neither had I held out any real hope of obtaining it.

I phoned Colin and we agreed on two courses of action. First, we would go and see the place. Some of us had had a quick look before, but now we needed to look through the eyes of faith. Second, we would meet together to pray.

We went to see Roffey Place the following day. It was amazing. As we walked round there was that sense of 'given–ness' about it. Colin and I looked at each other as we visited classrooms, bedrooms, houses, offices, kitchens, and all the other facilities. We had a common witness. If God were good enough to provide the means to buy this place it was certainly what was needed to fulfil our vision.

One thing I will never forget. We were taken to see the sewage plant. The incumbent caretaker seemed very

13

proud of the fact that the college had its own independent services, among which was the sewage plant. I climbed up the mound which covered the cesspit and turned round to look at Roffey Place. My heart was burning. I stood there and said a simple prayer, 'Lord, please give me this place'. That was in no sense a selfish prayer. I knew that Colin and I and the whole Bethany Fellowship would be involved in this, but I knew too that in a special sense I was going to be involved in a particular way.

Three years before this I had been invited to become Lecturer in Old Testament at London Bible College. That was a great privilege. It had taught me many lessons. I had given that up a year before because God had made clear to me in a very powerful way that he did not want me to be a teaching academic for the rest of my life. I had lived and worked in an academic environment for the past ten years and in that context I had found a new power in God through the baptism of the Holy Spirit.

I had left all that because of the conviction that God's call on my life was as a preacher. Revival, holiness and faith are the great themes that stir my heart. I felt the need to be available to the Lord without the restraint of the regular commitments and demands of a parish or teaching life.

Now here I was standing within the boundaries of another college.

On the next day, Thursday, Colin and I agreed to meet to pray. We met for a couple of hours in the morning and spent time waiting on God. We wanted direction about what we should do next. As we waited in prayer the conviction arose that we should go ahead, but the problem was the price. As we continued in prayer it was important that we gained some direction with regard to what price we should offer for the property. Colin stopped. He felt the Lord was saying we should offer five hundred and seventy thousand pounds. As we talked about that for a moment I felt that we should add another ten thousand to cover the cost of fixtures and fittings. From the human point of view both figures were ridiculous. For a start the agents had been clear that their principals would be unlikely to accept anything under six hundred thousand pounds. The other thing was that the fittings were worth much more than ten thousand pounds: after all there was a washing machine and dryer that between them were probably worth four or five thousand.

Anyway, we went ahead. Without a penny but girded by faith, we instructed Paul to compose the offer and submit it by nine o'clock the next morning.

A few hours later I was sitting round the lunch table with my family when the phone rang. It was Paul. He simply said that we had been successful in our offer. We sat in silence trying to assess the implications of that statement. I had been aware that there had been other offers, some of them from parties with resourses and reasons that made it very likely that they would have been successful.

It was the beginning of a great adventure of faith.

II

Testing the ground

It is amazing how one experience can so alter your life. That is true for many people. A bereavement, an illness, the challenge of a new job, falling in love: these are some of the things that bring about radical change and alter your whole perspective on life. This book is really about faith, but faith never operates in a vacuum. Faith has event as its context and becomes real in connection with the things that happen to us in real life. The purchase of Roffey Place was for me such an event. Before it I believed in faith and had seen God moving in miraculous ways through faith, but the experience of believing God for six hundred thousand pounds and the many things I learnt in those months of waiting affected my understanding of faith in a very deep way.

Faith has been lost in much of the church today. In many parts of the traditional and institutional church there is a lack of real understanding of faith.

I remember once not too long ago, I was asked to go and speak to one church meeting about faith. I tried to show how faith worked and what could be achieved in a congregation that would live by faith. We spoke together about spiritual goals and the reality of faith with regard to funds and fund-raising. Almost at the end of the meeting, after I had waxed eloquent about faith and given some clear examples of how God could work through faith, one dear lady stood up and objected to what I had said. 'It's all right for you,' she said, 'What we need to get is the money first, then we can have the faith!'

The church has no power because it has lost sight of what faith really is. Many people conceive of faith merely in terms of what they believe, but there is much more to it than that. Of course, it is true that faith has to do with what I believe. It is equally true that what I believe about God will determine what I expect of Him. What is not true is that faith is a set of opinions about God. There is an idea about in many quarters that one set of opinions is as good as another and that as long as we have some ideas about God then we are in the faith. Nothing could be further from the truth.

The Scriptures are very clear about faith in regard to what I believe. They call it 'the faith that was once for all entrusted to the saints' (Jude 3). In this sense the Scripture is the deposit of revelation by the Holy Spirit of the truth of God concerning Jesus. Faith is *the truth of Jesus expounded into my heart by the Holy Spirit*. Jesus himself said that the Spirit would not speak concerning himself but would take the things of Jesus and make them known to us (John 16.14).

The tragedy is that in much of the traditional church there has not only been a loss of the active sense of faith but of faith as the revealed truth of Jesus through Scripture. In many reaches of the church today it is popular to applaud pluralism. This means that you can believe what you like within certain broad boundaries and that each viewpoint is as valid as the next. No wonder the man in the street becomes increasingly unclear about the true content of the Christian message because he can go to an endless number of sources and get an equally varied view of what the gospel is. I believe that if anything is to be gained from the movement of renewal in the Holy Spirit throughout the churches today, it will only be ultimately valuable if it is allowed to challenge some of the views of Jesus that have become acceptable within traditional Christianity.

It is not an accident that people who have a real experience of the Holy Spirit in their lives soon begin to discover that they have new attitudes towards and beliefs about such important areas as the person and work of Jesus, the place and authority of the Scriptures and the significance and reality of sacraments such as baptism and Holy Communion. Many of these things have been unreal or unimportant within the context of traditional religion, but have taken on new significance and life in the light of a new experience of the Holy Spirit. This is easy to understand because the Holy Spirit is the voice of God who bears witness to the truth of all these things and who brings faith in them to life in our hearts.

The problem, however, is not limited to those parts of the institutional church which have been affected by liberalism. The full impact of faith has been diluted even within many evangelical churches. It has been land-locked into a once-for-all conversion experience. What has been lost is the ongoing dynamic of faith as it works in the daily life of the believer. It has become limited to putting our trust in Jesus. That is true as far as it goes, although even here we are sometimes left with the impression that the faith belongs to us and we have the natural ability to turn to God and trust him. The Scripture gives a very different impression:

'For it is by grace you have been saved, through faith – and this not from yourselves, it is the gift of God – not by works, so that no one can boast' (Ephesians 2.8).

I am sometimes asked, 'What happens then when a person does become a Christian? How do they put their faith in God?' I believe the answer lies in understanding the power of the Word of God. God is a speaking God and constantly he is making his voice heard within the experience of men and women. It may be through a Scripture or a preacher, but very often God speaks through quite other means. Sometimes he uses an event or a circumstance, sometimes a witness, far outside the bounds of traditional Christian witness, by which to speak into a person's life. Amazingly, a friend of mine, who is now a Church of Scotland minister, heard the voice of God through having a very bad trip on LSD. God spoke to him through the effects of that and in hearing the voice of God he turned away from his old life and began to seek another way. When we turn, that is repentance. At that point of turning God puts something else into our hearts – faith. As we turn from the closedness of our old way of thinking and listen to what God is saying, he puts faith in our hearts so that we can trust what he has done for us in Jesus.

But that is only the start. Saving faith gives way to living faith and God wants us to go on to find out how to live our lives through trusting him.

I firmly believe that one of the great spin-offs of the so-called charismatic movement has been the recovery of faith as a dynamic for life. It is not just doctrine, it is not just related to that first movement of Christian experience, it is a daily gift to enable us to live in the power and reality of the kingdom of God.

The trouble is that even within charismatic circles faith is being devalued. It has been cheapened by triumphalism. By that I mean that sometimes the impression is gained that faith is an easy way to God: that we only need to snap our fingers and God must do exactly what we want.

It is easy to see that the Scriptures are full of promises of faith. Jesus himself said that if we ask anything in his name
it will be done for us (John 14.14). There can be no doubt that many people live as though words like these were not in the Bible, but the question is how does such faith work? I hope this book might lead us a bit further towards an answer. The discovery I made is that faith is real. God does
want to answer our prayers. I discovered as well that faith does not work in a vacuum. It works within our hearts and lives and there are a great many deep lessons to be learned if we are to understand what faith really is about.

As I sat at the lunch table after the telephone call that told me that our offer had been accepted for Roffey Place, it was the challenge of faith that really hit me. What did I believe? How did I believe? We had no money, not a penny, towards the project. Not only that, but through my mind at that moment went a whole number of memories of people I knew or had heard about who had become involved in similar projects and who had subsequently either lost huge sums of money or had brought dishonour to God's name through stupidity. For a moment panic reigned.

Ultimately there are only two absolute tests of

prophecy. I recalled teaching that when I was a lecturer in Old Testament. The first is that, whatever miracle or wonder the prophet is able to achieve, he should not be listened to if he is not true to the revelation that God has given of himself. If he calls the people to worship other gods he is a false prophet (Deuteronomy 13.2). The second is that, if what the prophet said would happen does not happen, then he is a false prophet (Deuteronomy 18.22). These are two tests we need to bear in mind for our own day.

I don't think we should be frightened of such tests, nor should we think it faithless to feel our own human weakness when faced with great faith challenges. I would like to be able to say to you that I never once doubted, but it would be a lie. I would like to be able to say that the moment we got word about the college I felt absolutely secure and my heart leapt to faith. That too would be a lie. The effect in my own heart was to raise questions about where I stood with regard to faith. They were honest questions then, they are honest questions now. I believe the Scriptures are absolutely honest. What they proclaim is that if what we are handling is truly the word of God then nothing in all creation will prevent that word from coming to pass. Equally if what we are handling is the result of our own imagination then the result will be chaos, hurt and disillusionment.

Of course, this means that we must test the word, but it also means that we must proceed in such a way as makes room for God. The great danger of faith statements today is that of manipulation. You can make things happen to a certain degree and claim they are faith, but I believe that eventually such things will be seen for what they really are.

Where faith is pure, God will be able to go on working and the result will be fruitfulness. Where we have begun to manipulate events, the ultimate outcome will be confusion
and something less than God intended.

Through Roffey Place, I learned to wait on God to a degree that I had never known before. I can't say that I have got it perfect but I have learned and we are all learners. That is the heart of discipleship.

III

The deposit

We had four weeks in which to find the deposit, and the deposit for five hundred and seventy thousand pounds is fifty seven thousand pounds.

I wrote in my last book *HOW MUCH MORE* about the need always to take things back to the throne of grace. If God has given you a vision or a word, then the first place to test it is in his presence. After all, it was his word before it was yours. I like the Good News version of Colossians 3.15:

'The peace that Christ gives is to guide you in the decisions you make'.

The first thing to test was the reaction of our own spirits to the news after the initial shock. We spoke together as elders, we shared the vision with all the rest of the Fellowship. There was a great unison of spirit about it all. In my own heart I felt a great peace. At that moment I had no idea how God would provide the money even for the deposit, but I had that sense that we had entered into a real area of faith.

For me, the greatest challenge in relation to God is whether or not he still acts with power. I have no trouble believing in God from an intellectual or philosophical point of view, for while the idea of God creates certain problems for a thinking person in our world, the thought that he doesn't exist creates more. No, the challenge that goes deepest for me is the challenge of faith. I don't find it easy and yet I believe it is the most essential truth in the universe. I can put my trust in a God who makes his will known to me and who is able to provide everything that is necessary to live a life of trust in him.

When I looked inside myself I found that my response was still the same. There was a firm conviction that Roffey Place was what God had ordained and that he was going to provide the means to make it possible.

Apart from the inner witness of spirit there are other important witnesses to faith.

The Lord began to speak very powerfully through Scripture from a whole number of sources both inside and outside the Fellowship. The most powerful Scripture that God released came from a number of independent witnesses. It was a Scripture that came to me with great power.

As someone trained in biblical criticism, I was always taught never to take Scripture out of context. Indeed it has become one of the mores of evangelical faith that we must always look at the context. I myself have taught that for many years, but I believe the Holy Spirit often contradicts our most cherished traditions and he certainly did that here as he has done it before in my own experience. For a while after I was filled with the Spirit I found this hard to take. Everything about me had been trained to be cautious. As a Scotsman I have an inbuilt cynicism in my nature. My academic training taught me to work with a question mark much more easily than an exclamation mark. I believe there are many people like that today in the church who live under the influence of scientific scepticism even though they may not recognise it. In some ways that is a healthy thing as long as we recognise what we are doing and don't use it to quench the Holy Spirit when he decides to do it another way.

The scripture that God used was Deuteronomy 28.3:

'You will be blessed in the city and blessed in the country'.

You may consider the context to be quite appropriate anyhow from a spiritual point of view, because the words were first given to a people about to move into a great adventure of faith. The Israelites were standing on the plains of Moab on the far side of Jordan about to enter into the Promised Land. They had waited a long time for this moment, forty years in fact. It was lack of faith that had prevented them the first time at Kadesh Barnea.

The spies had been in the land for forty days and because the people disobeyed God they wandered for forty years in the desert: one year for every day. Now a new generation was about to possess the land. I believe there is a great lesson here. We can prevent God's purposes through unbelief and often God has to wait until the old unbelievers pass on before he can raise up a new generation who will trust him. That is why the continual cry of the Holy Spirit to the church is enshrined in the words of Hebrews:

'Today, if you hear his voice,
do not harden your hearts
as you did in the rebellion,
during the time of testing in the desert'.

(Hebrews 3.7,8).

It was not the context that was ultimately important this time, it was the words: 'blessed in the city and blessed in the country'.

Roffey Place is in the middle of the country. It lies one mile north-east of Horsham and four miles from The Hyde, the centre of fellowship life. More significant still is that we had just finished buying the old cinema down in Brighton which was being transformed into an evangelistic outreach centre. That was in the middle of a city. Still more important was the fact that the name chosen for the refurbished cinema was The City. It was to be the City of God, a place that would become a new Jerusalem for many who had wandered spiritually as well as physically. Today the City functions under the leadership of David Brown and inside, the coffee bar is called The City Gate and the restaurant and auditorium are called The City Square. But Roffey Place is in the country and God has promised his blessing in the city and in the country.

I looked for other confirmation as well. Together we felt it important that there should be some witness from outside the boundaries of the fellowship which would underline the fact that it was right to go ahead.

In the weeks that followed, gifts came from all directions, not because we advertised or put pressure on but because the Lord began to speak to the hearts of many people round about. Of course many people within the Fellowship knew of the project and supported where they were able. It was an amazing testimony of self-sacrifice. As the weeks passed so the amount of money for the deposit grew.

Colin left for a prolonged ministry trip abroad. He shared before he left that he felt we should take no firm step with regard to the deposit unless some witness came from outside the Fellowship that it was right. This was exactly as we had agreed and I felt that we should stand together in this whilst he was away. But it was not until the last day that I received the sort of witness for which we had been waiting.

Charles Sibthorpe, another elder of the Fellowship, sent me a letter over from the Hyde that afternoon. It had arrived earlier but had not reached me. It was from a member of a United Reformed Church in Cambridge. He knew that we were involved in some project but knew none of the finer details. His letter was the promise of a gift of about four thousand pounds. The only thing was that the money would not be available for about four weeks until the sale of his car had gone through. He felt, however, that the Lord was telling him to write the letter at that moment rather than later because he had a strong impression that this money was in some way to do with a deposit for which we needed money. It was as though the Lord had written the letter and my spirits rose.

Of course we still needed the rest of the money for the deposit. Indeed the amount that the letter had mentioned would have covered it nicely but the promise was there without the money. Another envelope was opened and inside was a cheque for the whole amount we needed save nine hundred pounds.

Time was running out since this was the final day before the deposit fell due. At first business next morning we needed to pay fifty seven thousand pounds if the deal was to go ahead. The phone rang. It was about fifteen minutes before the close of business. The voice at the other end was that of Maureen Budgen who had become a Christian only a few months earlier in the kitchen of my house where I was sitting. She announced to me that she had nine hundred and ninety five pounds for the deposit. I asked her where she had found it.

'Under the stairs', she said. What had happened was that Maureen and her husband had been helping a friend clear out her house. She must have been a bit of a hoarder because under the stairs they found a whole load of rubbish that had to be thrown out. Amongst all this stuff was an old shoe box and in the shoe box was nine hundred and ninety five pounds in old pound notes! Nobody knew if they were legal tender, but when they rang a building society they discovered that they could be traded in. The Lord had provided just the right amount at the eleventh hour plus fifty nine minutes. I sat at the kitchen table and felt quite weak. We were now in a position to take the next, but from the human point of view the riskiest, step, to put down the deposit and enter into contract with the RSPCA. Any mistakes from this point on would be expensive ones, a point which we were to prove in fact.

It is tempting to write this and perhaps to read it as though this is all that happened. This is the skeleton. Words will never describe the passion of faith, that feeling that is a mixture of assurance and intensity as you become aware that something big is on the move. It is something that is beyond your own capacity and it requires resources that stretch far beyond human abilities.

Apart from these few events, however, many other things were taking place at the same time. There was a tremendous witness of faith. All round the Fellowship people felt it was right. There was a sense of anticipation. God's people were on the move in faith because, in the language of the Old Testament, the Ark of the Covenant was on the move . We felt as though we were following God.

There was a great sense of fellowship in prayer. I believe these occasions can become a great stimulus to faith in the prayers of God's people. Certainly I became conscious of a great bouyancy in prayer. Through that people brought assurance and fellowship into the enterprise of faith.

As people waited on the Lord, the testimony of Scripture and prophecy increased. I think one of the factors that cheered me up the most was the comparative absence of 'prophetic word'. There is always a danger in moments like this to depend on an outbreak of prophetic activity. Personally I believe that prophetic words are much fewer than we imagine and that much of what is claimed as prophecy today is not really prophecy but encouragement and consolation. Prophecy calls for decision. A truly prophetic word calls people to God, provides a basis for repentance and always calls for obedience. Many words today are exhortation. In some senses we can take them or leave them without real, damage, but not so prophecy. It lays an obligation on people for obedience because usually at its heart stands God's next step of action.

One word that did come was very simple, but it was said with conviction. It was simply said that the ultimate provision for Roffey Place would not only come from this country but from abroad. The person who brought the word had no way of knowing from what source God would ultimately provide but it was that word that stood the test of time and, as we shall see, came to pass.

There was the reality of true sacrificial giving. One of the things that most moved me was the gift of a child's purse inside which was a pound or two in small change and silver. It was the savings of one of the children in the Fellowship who had been moved by God to save up all they had and give it to the Lord. The great thing about that was that it was not done under parental compulsion but because the child's heart had been truly touched by the Father through his Spirit.

One family in particular planted every penny they received into Roffey Place. They so believed that God had spoken that they committed themselves to stand in faith fellowship with me throughout the project. It got to the point where I could hardly give them money to live on but they gave it back to the Lord. 'Just another seed of faith', they would say. One day I will take time to see how many individual seeds they actually planted and how that related to the final outcome according to the principle of a hundredfold. For me it was a most amazing example of fellowship. Some of those seeds were planted on what for me were the most miserable days. I would be going through a period of darkness when through would come another seed of faith. At that time it was my own personal faith that such action fed and for that I was so grateful to God.

IV

Crucibles of faith

I was never any good at science at school. To this day the only image I retain in my mind of the old science room in Sanquhar Academy is of a bunsen burner and a small crucible, but that has, for me, become a most powerful image of living faith.

Some people seem to imagine that faith is something we have at the end of our finger tips which we wave like a magic wand to solve our Christian problems. Faith is not at all like that. Faith operates within human hearts. It is as we open ourselves inwardly to God that faith begins to work. The men or women who want to live by faith need to be ready to take within themselves all the challenge and cost of faith.

Paul rightly says that we have this treasure in jars of clay. God always works incarnationally. His plan of salvation includes and depends on the fact that it can work inside the lives of men and women. Any achievement of faith needs to be gained within the context of a human spirit. God creates us in the Holy Spirit to become crucibles of faith.

A crucible is a small vessel in which certain elements are put according to the experiment being undertaken. These elements are mixed together in the crucible and then the heat is applied from the burner. That heat creates a change. A fusion takes place between the different elements and an effect is produced. Perhaps a gas is released as a result of the intermix of the elements and the application of the heat. Whatever it is, the outcome is always the same. Use the same proportion of basic elements, apply a regular amount of heat to the crucible and the outcome will never vary.

Science depends on that regularity. Because of it, constant results are achieved and confidence can be gained in the practice of science.

It's like that with faith. Our spirits are the crucible. The person who wants to live by faith needs to be willing for God to internalize within him the basic elements he wants. For example, the first thing that comes to the heart of faith is the burden. God lays a particular burden on the heart to such an extent sometimes that it almost breaks. This is a principle that many people ignore or avoid, and because they do, they never discover the true effectiveness of faith.

Faith cannot operate without the basic element of the burden. This means that if we are determined to live by faith we will need to be willing to bear the burdens which the Father will lay upon our hearts. Quite often this will mean that there will be periods in our lives when it is evident that we are bearing a burden. This has nothing to do with human happiness or unhappiness, rather it is to do with feeling things as acutely as God feels them.

Sometimes the burden that is laid on our hearts has to do with our own life and experience. Because faith is operative at a great number of levels, from the deep personal level of holiness to the far wider level of burden for the world's need and lostness, the burden will vary according to our own place with God and according to God's will to use our lives as a crucible of faith. I don't think many of us come through to that place of being so open that the Father can use us in a profound way to bear his agony of behalf on the whole world.

The result of this burden being put within us is that it drives us away from the trivial into the deep. We begin to share the Father's concern or grief over the problem. The impact of the burden is to change our human response and to make us very aware of the divine response to the question. We begin to see and feel after the way the Father works.

In reality this burden of faith is a miniature of what the Father has already accomplished in Jesus. There in the garden of Gethsemane we can see the perfect man bearing the burden of God. It almost broke him and he knew the utter cost of that struggle. Drops of blood formed his sweat and fell to the ground. His spirit was torn in agony as he confronted the cost of the burden.

'Father, if you are willing, take this cup from me; yet, not my will, but yours be done' (Luke 22.42).

That day the burden placed on the heart of Jesus was the saving of the whole world. He became the crucible of faith to a degree we will never know, but I believe the principle is the same.

People must have wondered at the expression on the face of Jesus as he determined to do the will of the Father. The Scriptures say that he fixed his face like a flint to go to Jerusalem! (Luke 9.51). There was that determination of will that grew out of the burden that was growing on his heart. He felt the grief of his Father over a lost world. He began to see with awful clarity that to achieve the victory of faith 'the Son of Man must suffer many things' (Mark 8.31).

Paul knew that same victory of faith as he reached the conclusion of his work for Jesus:

'Therefore we do not lose heart. Though outwardly we are wasting away, yet inwardly we are being renewed day by day . . . we fix our eyes not on what is seen, but on what is unseen. For what is seen is temporary, but what is unseen is eternal' (2 Corinthians 4.16-18).

So to live in faith we need to be open to carrying the burdens of God. I believe it is this openness that will save us ultimately from trying to manipulate the vision.

As we live with something like this within our hearts we begin to see just how meaningful it is to the Father. If, for example, we are given a great vision of faith like Roffey Place, we need to understand in our spirits just how much the Father is in earnest about it. If the vision is really from the Father then we need to realise that he is much more in earnest about it than we are. If we begin to realise the cost of achieving such a victory of faith, then we need to understand that the Father knows much more about the cost than we do. Although the cattle on a thousand hills do belong to him and all the resources of the universe are at his command he knows full well that there are other problems to deal with.

For example there is the devious onslaught of the evil one as he seeks to divert the will of God. We must never underestimate this. There is also the fact that the Father has willed it that his resources are in the hands of men and women and it takes faith to be operative at many levels and in many lives for there to be the obedience that will release the resources. Now none of this is to undermine our faith in the Father or in the fact that he can provide what he wants when he wants. It is to recognise that from our human point of view God desires that we enter in with him to the depths of the exercise of faith.

Another real effect of bearing this burden is that we are delivered from triumphalism. Often when there has been a great achievement of faith, other people only see it from the outside. They imagine that people of faith only have to snap their fingers to obtain the blessing of God. Sometimes people are left with that impression by the way we speak of faith. We rightly emphasise the great promises of Scripture and the fact of the incomparable power of God – all that is true as we shall see – but the thing that tempers our triumphalism is the inner struggle of faith. If the truth be told, no great faith achievement has ever been wrought without struggle, and the struggle starts with the burden.

I know that as far as the miracle of Roffey Place is concerned, I lived with that particular burden for many months. It was almost six months in all and the year 1983 will forever live in my memory as the year of Roffey, not only because by the end of it God had released the funds in a miraculous way to buy it, but chiefly because of the burden of faith that was involved as we waited for it. I have never experienced anything like that. Not only did it bring deep spiritual change, but it had its effect in my personality and body. I came to see through that experience that it is a very, very deep thing to live by faith.

Of course there is more to faith than a burden. Another element that the Father introduces into the crucible is that of revelation. True men of faith are those who learn in the midst of the struggle to wait for a word from the Lord. It may be that this word will come directly through Scripture or by another impression as the Holy Spirit bears witness within our own spirit what the will of the Father is for the situation. What happens is that this word from God encounters the burden within our heart and an intermix begins to take place as the heat of waiting and prayer is applied. The word works on the problem and the outcome is that the victory of faith is achieved in a deep internal way long before perhaps it will be seen in practical terms by other people.

This produces a confidence of faith which is the outcome of the inner struggle before God. Those who have gone through this know the real meaning of Hebrews 11.1:

'Now faith is being sure of what we hope for and certain of what we do not see'.

An example of this took place in our experience of waiting for the supply of Roffey Place. It happened to Colin one night in Singapore during a ministry trip there. We were standing together in faith for the provision of the total amount of money. In the weeks before, something like three hundred thousand pounds had been supplied from many sources. It was a great miracle of faith. Yet we were still three hundred thousand pounds short. Colin had not had complete assurance of faith in his heart up until this moment that the money would be supplied.

Then as he was waiting on God in his hotel room the Holy Spirit spoke to him in a very personal way. He was given the complete assurance that the Lord would supply the outstanding amount and that in a particular sense he would be personally involved in it. In fact God showed him that some of the money would be given to him personally.

It was as though an angel had delivered a telegram straight from glory. The uncertainty departed and Colin was left with an elated spirit and the sure knowledge that everything was in the hands of Father. From that moment on it was as though he had the money in his hands.

Now this is a difficult thing to try and explain to people who may never have had the experience, but when I heard this account from Colin I knew myself that it was true. There was no way from a human standpoint that we could ever get that amount of money, but from then on we knew that God was going to supply the need. In fact, it was this word that led me later while we were still waiting, to be able to stand with confidence right to the very last day.

That is how faith operates. We open our hearts without reserve to the Father and he is then free to place within us whatever elements of burden and revelation he desires. These things mix within our hearts under the pressure of waiting in prayer and sometimes in the white heat of adversity.

But the result is the victory of faith. The man or woman of God can wait in the peace of God from that moment until the time of God's fulfilment.

V

Faith under pressure

Faith has to do with endurance.

It has to do with pressure. I find it significant to notice that according to Luke 18.8, what the Son of Man will be looking for when he returns is faith:

> 'However, when the Son of Man comes, will he find faith on the earth?'

I find it just as significant that such a statement comes at the end of the story of the persistent widow who gave the judge no peace until he listened to her case.

On a number of important occasions the New Testament speaks of faith in contexts that have to do with pressure or endurance. Sometimes that pressure takes extreme forms as, for example, in Hebrews 11.33ff:

> 'Who through faith conquered kingdoms, administered justice, and gained what was promised; who shut the mouths of lions, quenched the fury of the flames, and escaped the edge of the sword; whose weakness was turned to strength; . . . others were tortured and refused to be released, so that they might gain a better resurrection. Some faced jeers and flogging, while still others were chained and put in prison. They were stoned; they were sawn in two; they were put to death by the sword . . . the world was not worthy of them'.

When we see the faith to which we are called in a context like this it puts it all into perspective. Too often in the rich comfortable West, we associate faith with the meeting of our material needs. We see it as an easy way to fulfilment. Of course we have that promise in Scripture:

'My God will meet all your needs according to his glorious riches in Christ Jesus' (Philippians 4.19).

Personally I don't see any contradiction between the two because they are all subject to the provisional will of God. At any moment he knows what he is doing and he knows what is going to be most fruitful for his kingdom. Paul himself knew the secret of the all-surpassing provision and strength of Christ in every situation':

'I know what it is to be in need, and I know what it is to have plenty. I have learned the secret of being content in any and every situation, whether well fed or hungry, whether living in plenty or in want. I can do everything through him who gives me strength'(Philippians 4.12-13).

One of the greatest lessons I have learned through the Roffey Place project is the need to stand when under pressure.

After the deposit was paid we were given eight weeks in which to complete. Now that was a mistake from my point of view. I willl say more about that later. Suffice it to say for the moment that my wife had been very clearly told in spirit that we should complete somewhere around the end of September, which was twice as long as the RSPCA wanted. I understood their dilemma. They were keen for a completion because a previous sale, which had dragged on for a long time, had fallen through and they wanted to be sure of a speedy completion this time. Time was money as far as they were concerned.

I knew there were other important parties breathing down our necks and if we had withdrawn at that moment the property would have been sold to one of them very swiftly. Indeed, one party, a local broadcasting station had taken steps to obtain full planning permission to turn the place into a broadcasting centre.

Under the constraint of such factors I capitulated and agreed to a completion date eight weeks from the placing of the deposit. From certain points of view I suppose that was wrong. All I can say is that God used it to teach us some very deep lessons and to test our whole perception with regard to faith. I really do believe that some folk in the Fellowship had fallen into an easy-come easy-go attitude towards God's provision and the toughness of standing together for those four months or so really refined some of our ideas and brought backbone into many people's experience. I know from first-hand experience that many Fellowship members actually entered into this exercise of faith at a new and deeper level.

One of the interesting things that happened was that the pressure allowed us to ask serious questions about the actual property. Of course from some points of view it was too late, for by then the die had been cast. It would have been a very expensive business withdrawing from the deal at that late date, but for God nothing is ever too late. If we were wrong we were wrong, and we would have had to trust the Lord to get us out of the situation. The result was, of course, that the further we went the more we knew it was right.

Another interesting feature of that period was the temptation that arose to modify the vision. The vision of ministry we had was right of course, but was it the right place? I confess to having needed to ask for extra measures of grace on a number of occasions when that question was asked, because I had spent a long time before God and I was absolutely sure the place was right. For myself there was a theological issue. The vision and the place were intimately linked. I didn't see how, if this was the right time for the vision, it could be worked out apart from bricks and mortar, and had I not stood on top of the sewage plant under the impact of that conviction and asked God to give us that very place?

I allowed myself one experiment of faith. One morning the telephone rang. It was a member of the Fellowship telling me that someone had rung up from nearby. This person had read of our interest in Roffey Place in the local press and of our intended use of it. It so happened he had a property for sale for three hundred thousand pounds. That was just the figure we could muster at that moment. It was tempting to think that God had brought Roffey Place to our attention to raise our faith and to sharpen our vision and now here was the place he actually wanted us to buy having provided that amount of money.

Hilda, my wife, was unconvinced, because in her own spirit she was very sure that Roffey Place was right. I recall Caroline Urquhart saying to me not long ago that when she first walked into Roffey Place it had the same feeling for her as the very first day she saw The Hyde. There was a rightness about it that witnessed to her spirit.

Anyway we decided to pay the other place a visit. It was tremendous – part of a large country house set in magnificent grounds in a very strategic situation as far as travel and communication with the other parts of the Bethany Fellowship was concerned, but it was not right. It took me about two minutes to know that. The guided tour that followed was very interesting but equally frustrating because I knew we were wasting our time. The place God wanted was Roffey Place.

Recently, whilst I was preaching, the Lord brought a very vivid image to my mind with regard to faith. It was a memory from my boyhood days when, for a year or two, I worked down a coal mine in my native Scottish village. I worked among the lads who serviced the roadways underground and who kept the real miners at the coal face supplied with the materials they needed for their work. I remember seeing hydraulic rams placed in strategic positions as supports. They seemed dormant pieces of machinery, but all the time they were lying there they were keeping up the pressure. It was my job sometimes to check that pressure to ensure that it was sufficient for the purpose. If that pressure had been lost the whole support system might have collapsed. Now and again I read the dials and saw that everything was all right.

I might have paid no attention to those rams admidst all the noise and bustle of the active machinery down the mine. It might have seemed to a stranger that they were of little value or use, but they were vital to the safety of the pit.

It is like that with faith. Once we have started in faith we need to keep the pressure up. Faith is not a skip and a jump to glory. It is a building up of the pressure so that we stand right in there as God works his purposes out. God is looking for hearts that can take that pressure.

In the particular instance of Roffey Place I will always be grateful to David Brown. David at that time was fervently engaged in another part of the Fellowship's ministry and had great responsibilities himself. In fact the months that had just gone had been a time great pressure for David in his own work.

What happened was that the first date set for completion was due in August a week or so after the end of our great Family Week at Newark in Nottinghamshire. At the end of that week, which had made great demands on most members of the Fellowship and in particular on the leadership, a large number of people took some time off for holiday. My own household and I moved into The Hyde for a fortnight to see the completion through in faith. Nothing happened.

As the first week ran into the second, it became clear that if we were going to meet the completion date then the Lord would have to move very fast indeed, but there was no sign of any real development. I called the remaining members of the Fellowship together for prayer and David came over from the farm at Abbots Leigh to join me bringing one or two others with him.

During our time of fellowship a number of things happened. None of them were such as enabled me to complete the deal next morning and the contract went uncompleted, but all of them were faith building and by the time we had finished that meeting I knew more clearly than ever that it was God's intention to buy Roffey Place. As we stood together in praise and prayer under the intense pressure of a deadline we knew clearly that Roffey Place was absolutely right. We experienced a tremendous sense of oneness in the Holy Spirit and we entered into a deep mutual commitment to faith and trust. That night we prayed with power and reality and it was one of those occasions when you almost felt that a boundary was being moved.

I suppose that one of the most important things that happened for me through that pressure was that I came to see exactly where I stood with God.

It perhaps sounds very strange but I came to know very clearly that my faith and trust in God did not depend on a few pound notes but on what he has shown me of himself by his Holy Spirit in Jesus and by what he had done for me in sending Jesus to die in my place and be raised again for my salvation. Through this experience of pressure there was a great confirmation within of the absolutes of Christian faith and I knew the perfect security of being a son of God.

VI

The greatness of God

Faith rests in the greatness of God. Faith is founded on the sovereignty of God. The work of the Holy Spirit is to expound the greatness of God into our hearts. It is not something that is gained from 'News at Ten' or by paying a great deal of attention to surrounding circumstances. Indeed, this sense of God's greatness has often been experienced by saints in the most extreme situations of need.

Faith is founded on this experience of God that was the driving force behind many of the actions of the Old Testament believers.

Jeremiah stands out as an example. He was told by God to do a seemingly ludicrous thing. Just when the Babylonians were about to invade the holy city of Jerusalem, God told him to put all his life savings into a field in a small village just outside the city called Anathoth. It was, from the human point of view, a mad idea. There was no future in real estate; the bottom had fallen out of the market. Fortunately, Jeremiah was acting on a word he had received from God rather than on the approaches that were made to him by his uncle, Hanamel. His response demonstrates his awareness of the greatness of God. He knew that what seemed mad to man carried within it the ultimate purposes of God:

'Ah, Sovereign Lord, you have made the heavens and the earth by your great power and outstretched arm. Nothing is too hard for you' (Jeremiah 32.17).

Jeremiah was able with God's help to see beyond the immediate and enter into God's purpose for the future.

He knew that his field was a sign. He might never see it again, and tradition tells us he didn't as he perished at the hands of his fellow countrymen whilst in exile in Egypt, but it was God's sign that he had not finished with the Jews but would bring them home again from exile after many years and re-establish them in their own land.

This sense of the greatness and sovereignty of God pervades the Scripture. It flows right through the Old Testament into the New. After Pentecost it surfaced in the experience of the newborn church. After Peter and John had been hauled before the Sanhedrin and had been banned from preaching or teaching in the name of Jesus, the believers met together. They listened to the report of the apostles and then met together in prayer.

'Sovereign Lord, you made the heavens and the earth and the sea, and everything in them. You spoke by the Holy Spirit through the mouth of your servant, our Father David . . . Now, Lord, consider their threats and enable your servants to speak your word with boldness. Stretch out your hand to heal and perform miraculous signs and wonders through the name of your holy servant Jesus' (Acts 4.23-30)

This sense of God's greatness has led men and women to take immense steps of faith. Think of the example of Shadrach, Meshach and Abednego the friends of Daniel. They were hauled before the great king Nebuchadnezzer for failing to bow down and worship the image he had set up. Of course it was a trap, but that did not alter the seriousness of the situation. They either bowed down or burned to death. Their experience of the sovereignty of God governed their response to the king:

'O Nebuchadnezzar, we do not need to defend ourselves before you in this matter. If we are thrown into the blazing furnace, the God we serve is able to save us from it, and he will rescue us from your hand,

O king. But even if he does not, we want you to know, O king, that we will not serve your gods or worship the image of gold you have set up' (Daniel 3.16-18)

In the very last week before we had to complete the deal on Roffey Place a small incident took place that seems amusing to look back on but at the time it had fairly serious repercussions.

Our solicitor received a letter from the RSPCA. Over the previous two or three months they had been very patient and had allowed us to extend the completion date twice. That was not without its financial repercussions for us of course. It was clear however that their patience was running out because on the Monday of the last week this letter arrived. What it said basically was that while they sympathised with us they expected completion that week. After all, they pointed out, they did not have the same confidence in the power of prayer as our solicitor's client.

I looked at the letter in silence. I understood their feelings but it read to me like a direct challenge to divine authority. I confess that my blood began to boil. I was not mad at the RSPCA. I was just angry that someone should question the sovereign power of God.

I took the letter upstairs to my study and there I spread it before the Lord. I remember walking round my desk and more or less having an argument with heaven. After all we had stood in faith for four or five months by then. There had been a tremendous faith response to our prayers and over three hundred thousand pounds had come in towards the cost of Roffey Place. It is true that we were still just under three hundred thousand pounds short of the total needed to complete the deal. But nevertheless, I felt it was a challenge.

From the human point of view it seemed totally right. How, in the four days that remained, were we going to make up a shortfall of three hundred thousand pounds? After all, even with faith it had taken four months to get the first three hundred thousand. Yet over those months I had developed a tremendous sense of the sovereign power of God. I was not, at that moment, so concerned about the money. I was more concerned about the name of the Lord.

I waved the letter in the air and said, 'Do you see what they are saying about you, Lord? They are saying that you cannot fulfil your end of the deal by Friday'. I was filled with a great sense of power. I felt at that moment as though God in heaven had heard my cry and had taken note of the paltry cries of men. I could not have proved it from a logical viewpoint just then but I felt in my bones that God was going to act. In fact, as I look back on that period, I can say with truth, that although we shared many deep emotions and often felt very tired, not once did I experience anything approaching fear. Right through the project I felt a strange undergirding of the sovereignty of God.

Time and again the Lord has made Hebrews 11.6 live for me and this was such a time:

'Without faith it is impossible to please God, because anyone who comes to him must believe that he exists and that he rewards those who earnestly seek him'.

Actually, I have never been happy with the more modern translations of that text. The older Authorised Version says, 'must believe that he *is*'.

Now some might say that it is playing linguistic games to insist that 'he is' is different from saying that 'he exists'. That may be true from a linguistic point of view and there is no doubt that the modern versions are correct in their translation, but there are millions of people who believe in the existence of God who have never ever come to know within their experience the dynamic truth of his 'is-ness'.

Surely this is what Moses discovered in the wastes of the desert as he watched his sheep. For years he had accepted the existence of God, but here God drew near to him in a very different way. Here God entered the arena of his personal experience to a very different degree. Moses became aware of the 'is-ness' of God. When he enquired as to the name of God by which he could describe this experience the very name reflected the dynamic reality and power of God:

'I am who I am. This is what you are to say to the Israelites: "I AM has sent me to you" ' (Exodus 3.14).

Scholars have been deeply divided for years as to the actual meaning of the Hebrew term here. It is so sacred to Jews that they will not pronounce it. It is the Tetragrammaton, the four-lettered word that must never be repeated out of reverence for the God of whom it speaks. To this day pious Jews substitute another term which means LORD every time they come across the name in Hebrew Scriptures.

What everyone is agreed on, however, is that it is an active term. It is not a static description, but speaks of a living God, of a God who reveals himself in the lives of men and who acts with power within human experience. It is an exclusive name and it speaks of sovereignty. Often the question is asked of the God of this name, 'Who among the gods is like you, O Lord?'

This has always been the challenge of faith. In our lives, Satan is always trying to undermine the reality of God's greatness. If that can be extinguished then faith will no longer have a foundation on which to stand.

So important is this, I believe, that we need to see that it is this experience and knowledge of the sovereignty of God that prevents us from tying our understanding of faith into one experience or need.

Habakkuk is the Old Testament prophet who teaches us this most clearly. His little book betrays all the signs of a man who had come to experience, within his own heart, the greatness of God. He prayed fervently for the power of God to be made known in his own day:

'Lord, I have heard of your fame; I stand in awe of your deeds, O Lord. Renew them in our day, in our time make them known; in wrath remember mercy' (Habakkuk 3.2).

But his prayer is pervaded by a sense of the sovereignty of God. It is this sovereign power that convinces him that God is greater than anything or anyone else and therefore can hear his prayer for action in the present. It is this that also underpins his whole experience so that he is aware of the ultimate purpose of God:

> 'Though the fig tree does not bud and there are no grapes on the vines, though the olive crop fails and the fields produce no food, though there are no sheep in the pen and no cattle in the stalls, yet I will rejoice in the Lord, I will be joyful in God my Saviour' (Habakkuk 3.17,18)

This understanding of God is important to faith: nothing is too difficult for him. At the same time it points beyond the immediate problem as it did for Shadrach, Meshach and Abednego. Even if God does not do this particular thing, he is still God and in his sovereign wisdom he knows what he is about. It is this fact that faith trusts ultimately.

The experience of waiting in faith for Roffey Place had the effect of taking me beyond the immediate problem into a far deeper awareness of the sovereignty of God. I came to believe absolutely in his divine, exclusive power.

The great saints of the twentieth century, I believe, are not those like ourselves who have seen God's hand of provision in remarkable material ways. We do believe in God's power and we see the evidence of it in our lives, but that is because he wills it thus for the moment. The great saints are those who have so got to grips with the reality of God's sovereignty that they have been willing to stand in unshakeable faith even when it has become clear that the immediate context is going to be full of suffering and loss.

There are unheard of saints in China, Africa and other lands of overt persecution, where to confess Christ has not meant deliverance from the furnace. They have passed through the fire, but their unshakeable convictions about God have taken them there and they have persevered because they saw 'him who is invisible' (Hebrews 11.27).

Living by faith takes one beyond faith into God. That in turn creates faith because it makes us see the tremendous sovereign power and purpose of God in whom we trust.

VII

Echoes of faith

The exercise of standing in faith for something as big as Roffey Place is a maturing exercise. I began to find out things about myself that I never imagined were true. I am sure they have always been true but this period of time brought things to the surface in my own consciousness that were very challenging.

For example, I found out to a very fine degree how I reacted or responded to situations. I discovered facts about my own spirit that have become very useful in my ongoing development in ministry. I came to understand much more clearly what makes me tick and at which points I am fragile. I came to see the constants on which I act. It seems to me that God has made us like that. There are certain factors within each one of us that are constant. Given a situation of choice or decision I know the kind of things I look for inside myself much more clearly. It is on the strength of these elements that I find I act time and again.

I have a motor car that has an inbuilt computer for servicing. A series of five green lights is displayed on the dashboard and they show up according to what needs doing in the engine. If the car is in dire need of servicing only one green light shows and even that gives way to a bright amber, then red when there is danger. If everything is as it should be just after a full service then all five green lights show when the ignition is turned on.

It's almost like that with faith. I find that there are certain keys that turn when God is leading me into his will. I now look for these constants to direct my spirit in almost every situation.

I recognise the set of green lights that are the signs of faith for me. Each one of us needs to become sure of these things for himself for it is one important means of depriving Satan of his authority in our lives and of not being led astray by deviant voices.

The first signal for me is that of a *peaceful spirit*. It seems such a simple thing to say and yet time and again I have proved it true. I operate to a sense of peace. Often I have made a decision to do something or to buy something without that clarity of spirit and I have lived to regret it. I have found myself later trying to reverse the decision sometimes in vain but never without cost. The Good News version of Colossians 3.15 indicates that Christ desires to bring that inner peace to our spirits to guide us in our actions:

'The peace that Christ gives is to guide you in the decisions you make'.

Peace is God's amen to the movements of my heart.

I often work to spiritual hunches. I am sure there are other ways of describing such feelings but that is how I have come to know them. I receive a strong impression of spirit that such and such an action is right. That has developed over the years and it is governed by this principle of peace.

Just as it is true that evidence in church affairs must be in the mouth of two or three witnesses (2 Corinthians 13.1), so it is with regard to inner feelings. Hunches, impulses and inward guidance need to be corroborated by the peace that Christ gives.

The second signal for me is *my wife*. I am quite sure that half the time she is unaware of my reliance on her at this level but through the years I have come to appreciate so much her sensitivity of spirit in the realm of faith. She is a very different temperament from me and I find this useful in judging my own reactions and responses to any situation. She has a deep prayer life and I know that any important question that I ask will be asked by her before the throne of grace. One of the most important features of this is how well she knows me. Better than anyone else she is able to sift out the dross of my own personality before she comes before the throne of God with the question. I find it gratifying as I write this to be able to say that I know of no important spiritual decisions that I have taken in which we have had disagreement.

The third signal for me is the close circle of Christian *confidants* the Lord gives. There are a number of people in my life with whom I would share almost anything. They may not always be the same people for every situation, but I believe it is important for us to build up a mental file of our spiritual partners and be able to identify them in relation to our life with God. In the Bethany Fellowship of course, I share almost everything of import with my fellow elders. All of them are men who have lived through very deep experiences of life with God. An enterprise like Roffey would find its witness firstly among these men.

As we spent the months praying and searching for God's way with Roffey Place I found it very interesting to see how God used the different experience and personalities of the five of us who are Elders within the Fellowship. Among us there is a vast range of temperament and approach. It was a great experience to share together as the time passed and to be able to draw from each other insights and direction. In the life of faith it is vital that we learn to listen to others we can trust in the Lord. There is nothing more dangerous than maverick faith, thinking that we are sufficient by ourselves and have no need of other witness.

My experience is that the Lord provides checks and balances as well as encouragement and advice. To be able to sit together in praise and worship and to know that God was going to speak through that mutual experience was one of the most strengthening factors in the whole enterprise.

I find the experience of listening for the voice of God like hearing some great echo in a cavern. It starts with one voice, the witness of the Holy Spirit deep within one's own heart, but it does not stop there. It's almost as though the voice goes on and then the echo comes back.

These signals are, for me, the echoes of faith. I listen for the same voice coming back through these other people. As I hear the echo, I can recognise the same Spirit speaking, I can discern the same message. Sometimes it is strong, sometimes fainter, but always it is bearing witness to what has already been said.

As a preacher I have learned to sit on a platform before speaking and read these inward signs, often amidst a great deal of activity and other noise. Many of the preliminaries could be distracting to the word on my heart, but over the years I have learned to go deep within my own spirit and hold the word of God there. I have learned to listen for God within my own spirit in the middle of much other activity. I have learned to develop a sensitivity of spirit and to wait before God in silent prayer so that I know that when I speak it is God's word I am speaking.

This is essential for faith. It is necessary that we come to understand our own hearts. God speaks to our hearts, and deep within our spirits he can give that confirmation and assurance that no human being ever can.

This is especially important when we may be surrounded by a great many different voices. The one thing that is never in short supply in a faith enterprise like Roffey is good advice. The number of viewpoints is legion and so it is essential to know where you are with God in your own spirit. Of course this will not only be an individual exercise, so it is equally important to identify those close to you who have the same ability to hear God. Then you have the security of two or three witnesses.

I became convinced that part of the reason that the Father lets a situation be prolonged is to silence those voices that speak not out of faith but out of the flesh. Real faith has much more capacity to stay the course than the flesh and it is interesting to watch what happens as time passes. It is not only doubt and despair that changes mood: false enthusiasm evaporates like Scotch mist on a sunny morning.

It is also true that we need to discern the voice of God within the tumult of our inner emotions. I am never much afraid when it comes to faith, but there are other voices that clamour within our emotions that cloud the word of God. Sometimes anger, frustration, exhaustion or other feelings can dominate the spirit and threaten to close us to the voice of God.

I was brought up in a mining village. The village was set in a valley surrounded by high rolling hills. Quite often in the summer time we suffered severe thunderstorms. The fireplace in my bedroom was set into a corner of the room and through the night it often sounded as though the thunder was coming down the chimney into the room itself. In those circumstances I did what most ten year old boys would do. I wrapped the bedsheet round my ears, rolled myself up in the blankets and disappeared down to the bottom of the bed. I suppose I imagined that I was less vulnerable to the thunder in that position.

My father and mother were in the next bedroom and, of course, my sobbing did not go unheeded in the middle of the night. Now my father loved me a great deal, but he was not noted for his sentimentality. He would get up and throw open the door to my room. He would stand there cradled in the door frame with the light from the hall streaming past him. In his tough, gruff voice he would demand to know what all the fuss was about. Didn't I know that it was only a wee bit of thunder?

The effect was electric. I would shoot up from the foot of the bed and lie straight in the bed. After all, I reasoned, if my father could speak with a voice like that, what was a bit of thunder?

It's just like that in the life of faith. We need to hear the Father's voice. When he speaks he quells every other voice. He speaks with authority and whatever thunderstorm is sounding at that moment ceases to cause fear because he speaks.

VIII

The vision

The Roffey Place scheme did not start out as a search for a set of buildings. It was born long before that in the hearts of men who had been given a burden by God for such a ministry. We need to remember that, because there is a tendency today amongst many Christians to think that the Father will just provide six hundred thousand pounds or whatever according to our whim.

In the last few months I have been confronted by a number of Christians who have heard the story of Roffey Place and who themselves have wanted to pray for the provision to buy property, usually a private house. They have been surprised and sometimes distressed because their prayers were not answered. But faith is born of vision and I believe that we have Roffey Place today because for years that vision was being refined in the hearts of Colin Urquhart and myself. Quite independently we had carried for a long time the vision of a place where men and women could come for a prolonged period and be introduced to the principle of ministry in the power of the Holy Spirit.

I remember a few years ago approaching the authorities within my own denomination, the United Reformed Church, to see if they had any spare church plant somewhere in the country that could be turned to such use. The answer then was negative. I remember, whilst teaching within the confines of a more traditional Bible College, feeling the urge of spirit to have a place that would focus more on particular areas of ministry in the power of the Holy Spirit.

I have no desire to lose sight of the need for sound theological teaching or of the desirability of a good Biblical training, but over the years of my involvement in theological colleges, university faculties and Bible colleges I have become increasingly aware of the gap there is in our country for systematic introduction to the deeper areas of spiritual life and ministry. For a long time, I had felt the urgent need for a place where men and women could take time to explore these areas.

When I arrived at the Bethany Fellowship I soon discovered that my vision was shared by others. It was a spiritual dream that Colin himself had had for a long time. I felt in my bones that the time was drawing near when that dream would become a reality. The vision was simple. It was the vision of a place where men and women could learn about *faith*, where they could *experience* for themselves something of the power of God in their ministries, and where their *understanding* of deeper spiritual truths could be developed through study and fellowship.

Faith   Faith is the basic principle of the kingdom of God. Roffey Place came into being through faith. Those who come to study are able to share firsthand in a community of faith. They are taught to minister in the power of faith. They come to know the power of faith through prayer and involvement in the active faith ministries that operate in and through the life of the fellowship.

Faith is the greatest need of the Church today. Faith is what attracts unbelievers. When they see the evidence of God's power at work in human experience it is something tangible to which they can relate and which they can appreciate.

For too long our gospel has been all words. Even when we spoke of faith it was often only in terms of personal response to Jesus. That is valid as far as it goes, but what the Father wants us to introduce men to is faith as a principle of life, as a means of action. Faith is a gift from God through which we can gain the victory over the most difficult problems of our inner lives and experience. That is what John says in his letter:

'This is the victory that has overcome the world, even our faith' (1 John 5.4).

In our daily life as a college we live by faith. No applicant is ever interviewed in the light of whether they have the funds or not, but every person is taught to expect God to provide the means through faith.

Every day we meet together for three quarters of an hour to worship and pray. Often on the agenda is an item of faith. The whole body learns to stand together for every need and rejoices together in God's supply.

Experience   Experience is the greatest teacher of all. It moves us from the realm of theory into the realm of reality. Through it we can learn the actual power of faith and see at first hand the deeper principles of spiritual ministry in action.

This is how Jesus taught his disciples. He did not necessarily let them do the work: what he did was let them watch himself in action. Then, after a while, he was able to send them out by twos on a mission of their own. It is true that the real ministry of the apostles did not start until after Pentecost when they were endued with power through the Holy Spirit. None of us can minister without that. Yet during their time with Jesus in his earthly ministry, they had seen it happen. They had grown confident in the fact that where God's power was there would be God's event. They had no doubt seen Jesus and watched how he had brought men and women out and how he had responded to their needs in God's power. In short he had *discipled* them.

That is exactly what we need today. I know from my own experience the great benefit there is from spending time with other men who are experienced in areas of ministry that I have never entered into. Faith and confidence come from sharing and there is no substitute for being in a first-hand situation as far as faith ministry is concerned.

Of course, one thing we need to remember is that, at heart, ministry is servanthood. This is the greatest lesson we have to learn from Jesus. We need to recall the fact that he who is faithful in small things will be faithful also in much.

As I look back over the years, I can see clearly how the Lord has pressganged me into trivial service. He has been preparing my eye for detail and making me care about seemingly unimportant things. Too many of us want to run before we can walk. The Father wants us to develop gradually into maturity. One preacher said recently that whereas the Son of God spent thirty years in preparation for three years ministry, today we spend three years in preparation for thirty years ministry.

I feel today there is a great danger, especially in charismatic circles, of thinking that there is a shortcut to real preparation. I am aware of the shortfalls of traditional training schools for ministry, but the deep preparations of person and spirit that are necessary to minister in faith demand a much more rigorous school than any academic faculty.

It comes as a shock to some entrants to Roffey Place to discover that their first placement in ministry is with a broom and paintbrush or in some other mundane service.

Understanding Faith without spiritual understanding remains a very personal affair. To be able to minister faith into the lives of other people we need to come to an understanding of the way it works. We need to understand the power and promises of the Word of God, the operations of the Holy Spirit, the gifts of the Spirit and how they become real in our lives. Understanding is the key that transposes personal faith into ministry faith.

This means not only an illumination of the mind but an appeal to the spirit. It is when our spirits are quickened by the Holy Spirit that we can come to understand deep things of God that are otherwise lost to us.

One of the great tragedies of the modern western church is its dependence on pure intellect as a measure of faith. There is a sterility where intellect by itself dominates. I don't want to ignore the mind but I want to recognise that the mind itself is an area that needs to be subject to the renewing influence of Christ. That is exactly what Paul said in Romans 12.2:

'Do not conform any longer to the pattern of this world, but be transformed by the renewing of your mind. Then you will be able to test and approve what God's will is – his good, pleasing and perfect will'.

Where mind and spirit operate in harmony, being made alive by the Holy Spirit, the potential is enormous. Far from ignoring the powers of intellect this releases them. Of course it may determine that those powers are used in the service of faith rather than self or unbelief but we must never underestimate the power of a sanctified mind.

What we want to do chiefly, however, is to develop people's understanding of the operations of faith so that they come to a deeper knowledge of the ways of God in the power of the Holy Spirit.

'The Spirit searches all things, even the deep things of God. For who among men knows the thoughts of a man except the man's spirit within him? In the same way no one knows the thoughts of God except the Spirit of God. We have not received the spirit of the world but the Spirit who is from God, that we may understand what God has freely given us' (1 Corinthians 2.10–12).

In my boyhood I saw men who in human terms were completely unlettered, being educated in the power of the Holy Spirit. Some of them started their Christian lives hardly able to read or write but ended up teaching themselves Greek and Hebrew coupled with a staggering understanding of the Scriptures and of the ways of God. We need to believe for that kind of movement today.

One of the chief differences between those Christians who grow in their spiritual lives and those who don't lies in this area of spiritual understanding. Every Christian has an experience or experiences of God but some never advance beyond the subjective level. Others reflect, with the Holy Spirit's help on the meaning of these experiences and learn the principles of them so that they can pass them on into the lives of other people.

IX

The last chance

The phone rang. It was about ten o'clock at night and only a few days before the date for final completion of Roffey Place. This was our last chance, for already two dates had come and gone and the RSPCA had shown great patience. Now we were right up against the deadline with no way out. If the money was not there by Friday we would be in deep trouble.

Apart from any legal responsibility in a situation like this, there is the moral aspect. This is what I felt most because it seemed wrong to allow the Lord's name to be sullied in the eyes of men. I was very conscious of this fact as the last week dawned.

For the past two months we had been praying for the other three hundred thousand pounds, but there had been no movement and we had stayed in the same position for all of that time. Nevertheless there was a great sense of expectation. Only two days before, God had given my wife and others the same scripture from Isaiah 66.9:

'"Do I bring to the moment of birth and not give
delivery?" says the Lord. "Do I close up the womb
when I bring to delivery?" says your God.'

It was a very powerful word that brought peace and security into what otherwise would have been a very tense situation.

'Have you got it?' Colin asked. I didn't need to enquire what he meant. I knew only too well that he meant the money. 'No', I said, feeling a little shamefaced. After all it seemed a bit weak at this particular moment to have nothing else to say. He let me ramble on for a few minutes. I made some appropriate noises about being sure that God was going to work a miracle, that we all felt a great sense of expectancy, it was just a matter of timing and so on. It was all true but I doubt if it sounded quite as true as it felt. As a matter of fact I was absolutely sure that we were meant to have Roffey Place and that by one means or another we would take possession at the weekend.

By that time it had been decided that it was right for my own household to move from Tilgate Forest Lodge, into the big house beside the college at Roffey Place. It was clear that God was calling me to go, at least for a time, to set up the training centre and oversee the growth of the vision there.

I am sure that is another reason for the prolonged delay. It took some time for us to see just what was right and it took me some time to become resolved in spirit to yet another move and, in particular, back to another college. After all God had called me away from a senior teaching post in a Bible College only a year before and I felt a certain reluctance in moving back into that context.

'Don't worry', said Colin, 'I've got it'. I stood there rooted to the spot. I knew in an instant what had happened because I recalled the word of prophecy from a few months before which had said that funds would come from abroad to support this venture of faith. Nevertheless I found it hard to believe my ears.

Like most great movements of faith it was essentially simple. Colin had been on a preaching tour of Australia and on his return journey he had called into Singapore for twenty four hours to take a meeting. Whilst he was there he had fellowship with an old friend, a Christian businessman, but neither had spoken about the work and Colin had not raised the issue of Roffey Place. We have a covenant with God that when he calls us to a faith venture we do not advertise the fact.

Another friend of mine, Nick Cuthbert from Birmingham, was on that trip with Colin. I spoke to him after his return. He knew that day of the urgency back in

England with regard to Roffey and, in some senses, he felt the tension of the situation. He saw at first hand just how possible it is for God to move a person's heart without any prompting from a human agency.

Claire Urquhart, Colin's daughter, was with Nick Cuthbert on that particular trip. They had spent all day sight-seeing in Singapore while Colin spoke at some meetings. They returned to their hotel in the late afternoon to meet up with Colin but he never appeared. Time passed until there was only an hour or so left before they had to go to the airport. Colin arrived and whilst the others packed he had to rush tea with only half an hour or so left before the time of departure. During those few moments the Christian businessman asked Colin how things were at home. In the course of the conversation Colin mentioned the work and the need at Roffey Place. This caught the man's spirit because he went on to ask Colin how the money was coming in to buy the place. Colin then shared with him how the situation stood at that moment.

Without further ado, this Christian brother took out his cheque book and wrote Colin a personal gift for fifty thousand pounds! How God fulfils even the finest details! No doubt you will recall that in a Singapore hotel room months before Colin had received the promise of the money from God and with it the assurance that some of it would be given to him personally.

The brother then went on to say that the outstanding amount of two hundred and fifty thousand pounds would be in the Bethany Fellowship's bank account in England by Friday. At first Colin thought this might be some sort of loan or perhaps some arrangement made between a consortium of Christian business friends in Singapore, but

it soon became clear that this massive amount of money was as much a free gift to the Lord with no strings attached as was the fifty thousand that Colin had in his hand.

For Colin and Nick that was the longest plane journey they ever made back to England. Their hearts were burning with joy because they couldn't wait to share the news with the rest of us.

Surely the Lord had brought to birth in a spectacular and marvellous way. Just the day before I had received the letter from the RSPCA via our solicitors telling me about their scepticism. Here we were a day later with the promise of all the money by Friday. Praise God for what he can achieve in a twenty minute car drive to an airport.

Now I know how the Psalmist felt when he wrote the words of Psalm 138:

'I will praise you, O Lord, with all my heart; before the "gods" I will sing your praise. I will bow down towards your holy temple and will praise your name for your love and your faithfulness. *For you have exalted above all things your name and your word*. When I called, you answered me; you made me bold and stouthearted'.

The Psalmist is not saying that he will worship the 'gods' or recognise their validity. He is lifting up the name of the living God in front of all those enemies and opponents who seek to decry the name of the Lord.

That is just how I felt. I danced a jig round the room and praised the Lord for He had done wonderful things. I felt so strongly the reality of some other words from the Psalms:

'Not to us, O Lord, not to us but to your name be the glory' (Psalm 115.10).

We were not quite finished however. The bank draft was sent from Singapore to reach the bank in England by Friday morning so that the transaction could be completed. I made arrangements with the officers of the RSPCA to meet for lunch so that final details could be attended to. Their reaction, I think was one of pleasure and disbelief. They were obviously very pleased for themselves that the deal was likely to go through. They were equally pleased for us that we were going to be able to buy Roffey Place, but they could hardly believe that a cheque for two hundred and fifty thousand pounds was on its way from Singapore of all places to foot the bill!

Their incredulity was strengthened by the fact that, when Friday dawned and business opened at the bank, the money had not reached our end. It had got stuck somewhere in transit. I went ahead with the assurances that we were to complete although it was technically impossible at that moment. The officers of the RSPCA were slightly on edge and during lunch our solicitor phoned the Bank of Malaysia twice to check what had happened. In the end it was clear that the money was in fact with them in London but that it had not been cleared by the bank to our local bank in Crawley. In fact, we discovered that they were about to post a cheque by second-class mail which meant that it might be as late as the following Tuesday in reaching our own bank. That was no good. We made immediate arrangements for a messenger from the Fellowship to go to London to intercept that letter and bring the cheque by hand before close of business that day.

This was just another example of the need for faith from first to last. To live by faith is to learn the need to keep the pressure up. Satan wants to trip us up at any step, even up to the last moment. It would have been to the bank's advantage to have an uncleared cheque in the post over the weekend whilst that amount of money remained on deposit in their own vaults.

I was sorry for our friend the estate agent concerned in the transaction. He had been very helpful over the months and it seemed to him that there might be a last moment hitch. What was more he had made arrangements to leave immediately after that lunch for a weekend break in the west country. I assured him that everything was all right and that when he came back on the Monday the whole deal would be sealed up and his commission and reputation secure. I suspect, however, that it quite spoiled his weekend. I am not above thinking that the Lord wanted to use this situation to test these men with regard to their belief in him.

Faith is a great witness. It is not only the success of faith that witnesses to people around but the honesty of faith. At every point of the journey I had kept the agents informed exactly of our position and they travelled the road of faith with us albeit from a position outside of belief. We may never know what effect that had deep within their hearts, and I pray that God was able to work in their lives. All I can say is that they paid great respect to us and when everything worked out right in the end, I felt they were genuinely pleased.

X

For the sake of his name

One of the very real lessons that I learned from this whole
venture of faith was the fact that there are times when
God wants us to be willing to stand with him. We often
think of faith as God standing with us. He gives strength,
he brings provision, he opens the doors into otherwise
impossible situations. All this is true but there are times
when it almost seems to be the other way round. God
uses experiences like this to test our willingness to be
identified with his name above all else.

Sometimes I would be asked what I would do if God
did not provide the means to fulfil the contract on Roffey
Place. As a matter of fact, that never entered my head
once I had received that inward conviction of spirit that it
was right and as we continued to gather faith evidence as
to the rightness of the move.

If you are going to live by faith you need to be clear
that not everybody does that and at times you will hear
the voices of unbelief as well as those of encouragement. I
became increasingly aware that a great many people were
standing in the wings waiting to see what was going to
happen. This was made really clear when the local press
got hold of the fact that we were unable to complete by
the first date. It raised a whole number of questions
about what we would do.

The issue became very clear to me. I knew deep in my
heart that the Father was going to provide for the
purchase of Roffey Place in his perfect way. I also knew
that he was using this pause to test my willingness and
the willingness of other folks around me to stand for the
sake of his name. As time passed, that feeling became so

63

strong that I knew we were called to stand alongside the honour of the Lord. I was able to say in my spirit that I was willing to do anything on my side to enable the Roffey Place project to go ahead.

These choices for God are, I believe, an essential ingredient of biblical faith. Faith is not only about waiting for material provision for some project, it is about allowing God to take us deeper into himself and into ourselves. We see where we stand in relation to God in moments like these and I don't regret for a minute the fact that we were kept waiting beyond the first or second completion date. The effect of that in the lives of many believers was a strengthening of the resolve to stand with the Lord. We are his witnesses and what men think of him is a reflection often of what we think of him.

Time and again in the Scriptures we are presented with instances of this resolve. Think of Joshua confronted by a people about to enter into the promises of God, but who, at the same time, still carried their old gods with them. Joshua had to state his own position clearly and stand his ground:

'If serving the Lord seems undesirable to you, then choose for yourselves this day whom you will serve . . . as for me and my household, we will serve the Lord' (Joshua 24.15).

Elijah was in a very similar situation when he confronted the Baals on Mount Carmel. The people had a clear choice whether to follow the Baals or follow the Lord. Elijah introduced them to a very practical test. He initiated a faith crisis from which there was no escape. In fact, he made life doubly difficult for himself by allowing the priests of Baal to go first and then by dousing the altar with water when it was his turn to call down fire from heaven. But what mattered to Elijah was that he stood with God. At that moment everyone else was a mere spectator to the man of faith.

The same was true of Meshach, Shadrach and Abednego. Faced with the possibility of death by fire, they stood their ground. For them there was no concrete guarantee that God would deliver them. They felt this would be the case, but even if God chose not to they were determined to stand with God and be identified with his name, and they let the king know this in no uncertain terms.

So it was with Daniel. In fact, you might almost say that Daniel precipitated a crisis of faith because of his determination to stand with God. After hearing the contents of the decree that had been passed prohibiting him from praying to the living God, he deliberately set out to make his position clear. He went to his house and threw open his window and three times a day he prayed towards Jerusalem. This was a very public act of defiance that could not go unheeded, but for Daniel it was an important witness to the fact that he stood with God.

The same testimony passes through the Old Testament into the New. The first preachers, Peter and John, made the very same sort of stand when they were prohibited from preaching in the name of Jesus according to Acts 4. Hebrews 11 makes it clear that not everyone who has made such a stand has enjoyed deliverance in an immediate sense. Sometimes their stand with God has cost them everything, their possessions, their friends and even their lives.

The 11th of August had been fixed originally as the date of completion. In retrospect I know that was a mistake. That date and two others were to pass before we could ultimately complete on October 7th. We learnt a lot of lessons about sticking to the Lord's timetable instead of being pressured by plans of man!

Nevertheless, the waiting did us all a lot of good. It sorted the men out from the boys. I don't think any of us who were involved closely in that prolonged period of waiting will ever be the same again. God used this time of waiting for radical pruning. A false triumphalism that wants answers without cost was challenged; a rose-coloured spectacles view of life in which everything comes easily was altered for many people. We learned the cost of faith.

During this time God gave me a verse of Scripture that proved a tremendous blessing and strength. It comes from Proverbs 20.21. I don't think I had ever noticed it in my Bible before!

'An inheritance quickly gained at the beginning will not be blessed at the end'.

Those words confirmed the growing certainty that the Lord was going to vindicate his name and perform a work that would astound saints and confound sceptics.

It was at this time that I learned the need to stand with God. I was so troubled by some of the adverse comments that were being made in various quarters that I determined in my will to be identified with the name of the Lord. The local newspaper had run an article about Roffey Place, which made it clear to all and sundry that we were still not in a position to complete even although they presented it in a way that was thoroughly sympathetic to our predicament.

Colin was away and so I called together not only the remaining elders, but some leading brethren in the fellowship who could be relied on to share their hearts honestly. I shared my position and how I felt that we needed to be responsible on behalf of the Lord. We all agreed that the money was going to be provided by the due time and in a miraculous way, as the first three hundred thousand had been provided.

What we also agreed was that we needed to be in a just position as far as those on the other end of the deal were concerned and as far as other Christians round about were concerned. We agreed together to approach the bank to provide a bridging loan until such time as all the money had been provided. Two major banks declined to help. Then a contact opened up remarkably with a merchant bank in the City of London.

Some of us met with officials from the bank who listened intently to our story. It was a tremendous experience, first to speak with the world at that level about a venture of faith and second to discover that they were sympathetic to our cause. During the discussion I made it clear that I felt the facility would not be required and shared with them the reasons for our approach. They were perfectly amicable and in the end made us the offer of help on advantageous terms.

I drove away from that interview feeling strongly that this was not the way God was going to use to meet the need, but feeling at the same time that in some mysterious way we had stood with the Lord. Come Friday the money would be available from at least one source to complete the deal with the RSPCA.

This was a lesson the Holy Spirit had taught me throughout the whole summer. The book that helped me time and time again and which I read at least three times through was *REES HOWELL: INTERCESSOR*. It amazed me to see time and again how God had done in that man's experience precisely what he was doing in mine.

The merchant bank broke all records in preparing the paperwork to make the money available in time. I had the joy of being able to ring them on the Wednesday morning following and telling them we did not need their money. The work they had put in on our behalf cost us four hundred pounds but their attitude when they heard of God's provision was very gracious and warm.

The words of the Lord to Eli and his sons ring with new power within my heart as a result of this experience:

'Those who honour me I will honour, but those who despise me will be disdained' (1 Samuel 2.30).

XI

Solitude

At the heart of faith stands a certain kind of solitude. The man of faith needs to know what it means to be able to stand alone. This is no contradiction of the fact that many other people may be standing alongside him for faith. It is simply the recognition that faith calls for an apartness of spirit at its deepest moments which no other human being can penetrate. It is through these times that we come to know the presence of the Father who alone can share that solitude with us. He shares it because he knows it.

Some words of Oswald Chambers on the very subject came home to me recently:

'A servant of God must stand so much alone that he never knows he is alone. In the first phase of Christian life disheartenments come, people who used to be lights flicker out, and those who used to stand with us pass away. We have to get so used to it that we never know we are standing alone'.

There is a true loneliness about the life of faith. If we are to stand in faith we will need to recognise that, although we will be with *people* there is a deeper sense in which we will be *apart* from them.

Oswald Chambers is highlighting an important fact, of course, that when we get through the human feelings of hurt or disappointment or tension that often accompany this experience of loneliness, we come to that stage of finding Christ at the heart of it.

I was travelling along the other day and my eye fleetingly caught sight of a slogan on a roadside board. It said simply, 'JESUS NEVER FAILS'. That is the discovery of solitude in faith, but it is a lonesome journey for a soul and it passes through more than one personal Gethsemane to reach it.

The Gospels bear witness to the fact that Jesus knew this experience many times. One thinks of the occasion when he came down from the mountain to find his disciples in difficulty over the case of a boy who was possessed by an evil spirit. The incapacity of the disciples had become an occasion for wrangling amongst the opponents of Jesus. You can almost taste his frustration with them in his response:

'O unbelieving generation, how long shall I stay with you?' (Mark 9.19).

It was the fact that Jesus knew and understood more about the ways of the Kingdom of God than his friends that set him apart.

At other times it was the need to grapple at a very deep level with the issues involved in his mission. The outstanding example of this must, of course, be Gethsemane. Matthew captures the pathos of that aloneness when he reports the words of Jesus:

'My soul is overwhelmed with sorrow to the point of death. Stay here and keep watch with me' (Matthew 26.38).

A struggle was taking place within the heart of Jesus and others could only be onlookers. He asked them to be nearby to pray and surround him with the protection of fellowship. Sadly, they failed him at this most crucial moment, but then that is hardly surprising from one point of view. My experience is that few people can enter into another person's spirit at a time like this and often their reaction is to withdraw in something like embarassment because they do not properly understand what is going on.

There were many other reasons why Jesus found himself set apart at times even from his most intimate

69

circle of disciples. Sometimes it was his sense of utter commitment to the commission which the Father had given him. The others never seemed to have quite grasped the depth of that. Remember the exchange between Jesus and Peter as Jesus tried to intimate the absolute cost of the mission to them:

> 'He then began to teach them that the Son of Man must suffer many things and be rejected by the elders, chief priests and teachers of the law, and that he must be killed and after three days rise again' (Mark 8.31).

Peter took the lead as usual in their response to this. He began to rebuke Jesus, but Jesus had to deal sharply with him and introduce him to the reality of faith. If God's purposes are to be fulfilled then it calls for men willing to bear the cost of that within themselves.

There are other hints you could never prove but, as you read the Gospels, you are left with the distinct feeling they may well be true. Take, for example, the relationship of Jesus with the home at Bethany. That was a special place for him; it was the home of three dearest friends. They seemed to stand in a special relationship with him and yet they were not included in that inner circle of disciples. There seemed to be a deep affiinity of spirit between Jesus, Lazarus, Mary and Martha. One can only speculate what that affinity might have become perhaps, in particular with Mary, if the Son of Man had not been walking that lonely path of faith in his Heavenly Father. He had not come to do his own will but the will of the one who sent him. Of course, nowhere is this more clearly seen than in the suffering of Calvary. The solitude there can never be plumbed. It is concentrated in that cry of agony that is squeezed from the spirit of Jesus as he echoes the words of Psalm 22:

> 'My God, my God, why have you forsaken me?'

There is the dereliction of faith at its deepest. He had trusted the Father absolutely, even unto death. Now, it seemed to Him that even the Father had deserted him. Of course, that was not absolutely true, but the Father had to stand by and watch as the plan of salvation took its course. Only at the right moment could he demonstrate his ultimate care for the Son he loved.

What solitude must have struck the Father's heart at that same moment. Never had there been dislocation of spirit between them. Now the saving of all men demanded the breaking of that which was most precious. The words of the hymn we know so well can only grasp after the depth of that alone-ness:

'None of the ransomed ever knew,
How deep were the waters crossed,
Or how dark was the night that the Lord passed through,
Ere he found the sheep that was lost'.

None of us can ever know solitude like that, but it is a great forerunner for every man of faith.

I have discovered the reality of this in the last year or so. Before ventures like Roffey Place, I thought I understood something about faith. I identified it chiefly with believing. Now I believe faith has to do much more with being. It is not just a claim of promises that have been made, although it includes that. It is a process that comes to birth and fulfilment within a person's spirit. That is what Oswald Chambers means when he speaks of the movement that takes place until we become so aware of the Lord's presence with us we do not realise that we stand alone at a merely human level.

I am writing these words in the lounge of a hotel on the island of Jersey. I am surrounded by the world on holiday. Nearby is a group of older people discussing the vital issues of the day that captivate their interest. Today they are consumed by speculation of who will win the current snooker championship on television. It makes me realise how trivial it has all become to my spirit. An experience of faith like Roffey Place leaves a deep mark on the soul.

After faith, much of life seems trivial. There is a loneliness in that. The world whirls around full of its own interests and theories. It is consumed with the importance of time and sense, and all the time you sit there knowing the privilege of having touched a deeper reality and feeling a profound sadness and unease of spirit with things as they are.

How Jesus must have felt as he made his solitary way to the fulfilment of the purpose of the Father. I don't suppose his world was that much different from ours. Men lived for time and for themselves. Today we are that much more aided by machines that help us still further towards self-indulgence. For Jesus, life had a much deeper meaning because it was time spent in the light of eternity.

There are moments when, for faith's sake, God closes us in with himself. At that time it perhaps does not seem a very pious experience or to have much to do with faith. But the Father deals with us in deep and personal ways and he uses implements to fulfil his purposes that we would never dream of.

One lesson learned this last year was that God develops within us such a sense of purpose that it often threatens to overwhelm us. It cuts us off from other people, but that sense of purpose drives us into faith because the more we experience it the more we realise that it will never be achieved unless the Lord does some marvellous things. It can be terribly frustrating when other people don't seem to share that sense of purpose or when they attempt to deviate your interest on to more passing considerations. My experience is that men of true faith live with faith issues before their eyes all the time and find it difficult when their attention is drawn away to something that may be very legitimate but, in the light of the issue in hand, will seem completely trivial.

Of course, there come those periods when, as Jesus experienced, faith demands a deep wrestling and agonising of Spirit. This struggle is often necessary to clarify the vision. It is only in such depths that we can perceive the truth. Sometimes the struggle is necessary to separate us from all the other items which engage our interest, so that within the wrestling we can find direction and know what steps are right to take.

I even found that God used those times of physical weakness and exhaustion to achieve his purpose. Some folk want, in kindness and sympathy, to remove such experiences completely, but they are the hand of God. I know from my own experience that I have become so aware of my own frailty that it has cast me utterly on God. Apart from that, my own human exuberance and push would be liable to take over the exercise.

Why does the Father allow these times of solitude? Through the experience of standing in faith for Roffey Place I came to recognise certain important elements in this.

Firstly, *it breaks the mould of our old life.*

As the months have passed I have found myself asking the question whether I will ever be the same again. So deep is faith that it brings about changes even in our personalities and certainly in our perspectives upon life. What has changed for me is my conception of joy. In faith, superficial happiness must give place to divine joy. Happiness takes its note from the present, joy takes its note from the future. That was surely the secret of Jesus's own faith.

'Who for the joy set before him endured the cross, scorning its shame, and sat down at the right hand of the throne of God' (Hebrews 12.2).

Secondly, *it refines the vision in our hearts.*

To see clearly and think deeply we need the quiet of solitude. If we are to concentrate on the vision of God we need to be brought into a place where our whole spirit can be taken up with that vision. Nothing must distract us or divert our attention. Moses was closed in with God when he received the words of the Law on the mountain. The result was that other people could perceive the glory that had come to his face because he had been alone with God and nothing else had been allowed to interrupt.

Thirdly, *it deepens our relationship with the Father*.

Especially the Father – not just God in a more general sense, but the Father. For there we come to know he loves us and there we grow to trust and understand his spirit. There is a whisper of divine love at the heart of faith. It is a special word that is given to every person who will allow himself to be shut in with God. Let me be clear. I don't mean that we necessarily need to spend hour upon hour physically by ourselves with God. This shut-in-ness is something that operates at a very deep level of spirit. Often we can go about the demands of daily life and still remain shut in with God.

But we come to know God as Father. There he loves us and there he reveals to us his will. This is the secret of Oswald Chamber's words which I quoted at the beginning of this chapter. The Devil wants to prevent us from breaking through to this communion of spirit. He wishes that we stay in the solitude with no sense of the Father. Then we will be crushed and our spirits will descend into despair, but with the Father, there is no fear:

'There is no fear in love. But perfect love drives out fear' (1 John 4.18).

Fourthly, *it sharpens our sense of values*.

Time and again Scripture portrays believers as a pilgrim people with their eyes set on the horizons of God's ultimate plan. The great father of faith himself, Abraham, is portrayed like that in Hebrews chapter 11. He went out, not knowing where he was going, but he was looking for a city whose builder and maker is God. That's faith!

True faith is prophetic. It not only declares what is, it looks for that which is not yet. It has its eyes set on God's horizon, not in some vain hope that something might happen but in the assurance that it will, because it has had an intimation from the Father. It may not know everything but it knows enough to expect that God is about to perform his will.

I am certain there are many other lessons to be learned from the solitude of faith but these are some of the important things that I have come to know through it.

Faith is a prophetic experience. It stands in the midst of life as a divine contradiction. It calls us to exploits and values that seem strange to normal human experience. In fact it cuts us off from normality. Better still, it introduces us to another sort of normality.

This is the normality of trusting God, of recognising the Father, of following a vision of another world that challenges the triviality of the here and now.

XII

The crossroads of doubt

'Stand at the crossroads and look; ask for the ancient
paths, ask where the good way is, and walk in it, and
you will find rest for your souls' (Jeremiah 6.16).

At the end of chapter two I indicated that I had suffered
doubt in this experience of standing in faith for the
provision of Roffey Place. It became much more than
that. I not only experienced doubt, I feel that to some
degree I came to understand it.

What we need to understand is that doubt is not the
opposite of faith. Doubt can certainly become a threat to
faith, but unbelief is the opposite of faith and doubt is
not thoroughgoing unbelief. Doubt is a sort of no-man's
land between faith and unbelief.

Doubt is faith under pressure. Sometimes it is faith
suffering from malnutrition or ill-treatment. Doubt is a
shaking of the foundations and, depending where we
proceed from that point, we will end up either in faith
or unbelief. Where doubt is real, it is not the superficial things of life that are under attack so much as the
very pillars and foundations of our personalities and
faith.

Satan wants to take our doubts and drive us into a
wilderness of unbelief, a sterile place where we have no
joy and where the power of God is never seen. So we need
to be aware of the danger of doubt. Faith that never
doubts is not real faith, it is some kind of false triumphalism, because I believe the Father takes our experiences of
doubt and uses them for our maturing and for the testing
of the faith that he puts within us. Doubt is the furnace

in which the dross is burnt away and in which the pure gold of God's word endures.

I came to recognise a number of important features about doubt through this great faith experience. Many of these features can be illustrated from Scripture, from the lives and experiences of other men and women of faith. Of course what we need to see at the outset is that faith passes through doubt. It does not remain there because then faith itself would become sterile and be lost.

TWO ELEMENTS. Where there is doubt there is always more than one element involved. Doubt arises when more than one point of view is introduced or more than one opinion listened to. This is a major reason why the Devil is so concerned to surround people of faith with a whole number and variety of views. It creates imbalance and without the gift of discernment from the Holy Spirit it becomes difficult to make a choice between one opinion and another. This is why true faith never operates at the level of opinion but of revelation. It is not that it does not listen to what other people are saying, but all their views need to be heard and judged under the impact of the word that God has given.

This idea, that God is able to speak specific words into particular situations in an immediate sense, is something that has become lost to great reaches of the church today. We have settled down with a religious democracy where what is heard is the voice of the mob (that is what *demos* means) rather than the voice of God.

We only have to look at some of the Greek words of the New Testament which have been variously translated by the English word 'doubt' to observe this principle of there being at least two elements present where there is doubt.

Take for example *James 1.8*

'He is a double-minded man unstable in all he does'.

The idea present in the word *dipsuchos* is of the man having two souls or hearts. His affections are torn in two directions. Instead of sticking with one option, in this case trusting God, he listens to other voices. The result is an inner instability of spirit that leads to an immaturity of person.

Take again *Matthew 14.31*

'Immediately Jesus reached out his hand and caught him "You of little faith," he said, "why did you doubt?"'

Peter succeeded as long as he stood on that word but whenever he began to take more notice of the violence of the wind rather than the word of Jesus he began to sink. The word that is used to report the response of Jesus is *distazo:* 'You of little faith, why did you doubt?'

In essence the word means to stand in two places at once. Every one of us knows the tension that rises in our spirits when we try to stand on both sides of the fence at once. In the immortal words of Abraham Lincoln, 'It may be very nice but it soon becomes very painful'.

Or look at *Luke 24.38*

'He said to them, "Why are you troubled and why do doubts rise in your minds?"'

Here the disciples are amazed at the appearance of the risen Jesus amongst them. At first they thought they were seeing ghosts, but Jesus put their minds at ease by showing them his hands and feet.

'Why are you troubled, and why do doubts rise in your minds?'

The basic idea is of disputing or arguing. The doubts arise because there is more than one view on the matter and an argument ensues.

Often when we are called to stand in faith over a specific issue, we will find that the Devil becomes the great disputer. That was his role at the very first. He came to the woman in the garden and he cast doubt over what God had actually said.

Time and again during the Roffey Place enterprise we found it necessary to go back to the first words of direction and promise the Father had given us. At times the issue was in danger of becoming clouded by other points of view. It is essential for faith to see that not every word that is spoken has equal value. Every word needs testing against the first word that God said in the situation.

It is similar to Mark 11.23 where yet another Greek word is used. This is where Jesus instructs his disciples about faith:

'I tell you the truth, if anyone says to this mountain, "Go throw yourself into the sea", and does not doubt in his heart but believes that what he says will happen it will be done for him'.

The word here is *diakrino*. It means 'two judgements'. That is exactly what Jesus is saying. We are either to take his word or someone else's word for it, but there can be no divide. The thing that makes faith inoperative is the division that comes through doubt.

There are a number of other examples we could look at, but these are sufficient to establish the principle that most of us would recognise from experience. That is, that doubt is division.

Now that is not fatal, if what we do is respond to doubt with the help of the Holy Spirit, because then the Spirit will take doubt and make it creative in our lives. We will be led by the Spirit through the wilderness to hear again the word of God. What is fatal is if we close ourselves up against God. That is the great danger of doubt, that by it our hearts will become cold and our minds cynical and we will allow ourselves to be led away from that place where we can hear again the word of God.

I have found with doubt that the best thing to do is wait. Satan wants us to panic because of doubt, but doubt, by itself is no reason for panic. What we must do is wait and keep our hearts peaceful until we are in a state to hear the voice of the Father again.

SPIRITUAL EROSION. Doubt is erosion. It is something that nibbles away at our securities and fundamental beliefs. That is why it can go so far before it is recognised. Many people suffer from real doubt and the damage it can cause before they know it, because it is a gradual thing.

Doubt is first an erosion of our inner being. There are many things that can be the cause of this. The surprising fact that few Christians seem to recognise is that it can be the very goodness and busyness of our enterprises of faith that lead to doubt. We become tired and weary inwardly and we begin to feel that one more item will break us. If we go on like that, it will not be too long before we have not the capacity for faith. Praise becomes tired, prayer becomes tired, fellowship is tiring, and all the strong pillars of our faith become a chore. Instead of listening to the word of God within our lives we begin to listen to ourselves. The negative takes precedence over the positive until we arrive at the state where we are no longer quite sure what we believe.

That great preacher, Dr. Martin Lloyd-Jones, put it very well when he said that doubt comes from listening to ourselves rather than talking to ourselves. God has given us many words of faith with which to preach at ourselves. We need to learn the pratice of this if we are to prevent the erosion of spirit that stands at the heart of
doubt.

Also involved in doubt is our view of God. Time and again in Scripture, the people are challenged with regard to their view of God. Joshua demanded of the people that they chose whom they served. He had made his mind up, he and his household would serve the LORD.

Elijah posed the very same challenge to the people when they were tempted to follow the way of the Baals. On Mount Carmel he presented them with a most effective visual aid of the power of God. Not content to make the claim that God was able to do what he said, Elijah first gave the other side the chance to prove their own claims on behalf of the Baals.

'Elijah went before the people and said, "How long will you waver between two opinions? If the LORD is God, follow him: but if Baal is God, follow him"' (1 Kings 18.21).

Faith operates with a high view of God. It trusts the Father who acts in power through the Spirit. It looks to Jesus because in him it sees and hears the irrefutable voice and word of God. Faith does not put its trust in a pipedream but in the living God whose 'arm is not too short to save, nor his ear too dull to hear'.

Satan's interest in our lives is to diminish our view of God. In the church today he is having a field day on this front. At the moment of writing the discussion is raging once again around whether we can or should address God as 'Our Mother'. Such ideas are not only blasphemous, they are an offence to faith which sees God neither as mere man or mere woman but through the prism of divine revelation. Faith sees God as he has revealed himself, as he has chosen to speak of himself. Male language in relation to God is never interpreted in a sexist way by faith, but as a means of communicating the greatness, the authority, and the compassion of a loving Father. It perhaps should come as no surprise to us, in a society where these very human values are so undervalued, that man's view of God should be so distorted and low. J. B. Phillips was right when he once said, 'Your God is too small'. That is the epitaph of modern religion without revelation.

Faith cannot operate in that atmosphere and where our view of God is miniaturised into our own image, then our capacity for faith is likewise lessened. It is only when men and women operate with a high view of God and take heed of what God has shown of himself that they can in any real sense live by faith.

Another area of erosion is in our memories of faith. Since the beginning, God made sure that in the corporate life of the Israelites there were those ceremonies and liturgies that caused them always to remember the mercies of God. We have one example of this in Deuteronomy 26.5, where the people repeat the words during the feast of firstfruits:

> 'My father was a wandering Aramean, and he went down into Egypt with a few people and lived there and became a great nation, powerful and numerous'.

The purpose of this and other recollections was to ensure that God's people never forgot what he had done for them in their past. This kept them from complacency and reminded them of the covenant that stood between them and the Lord.

One of the main things that kept my faith alive during the Roffey Place project was the memory of all that the Father had done in the days that had gone. Why only twelve months before, we had moved into the very house we were living in, as a result of a great move of faith when God provided a hundred thousand pounds to make it possible. This amount was a huge sum to me and the memory of that drove me forward in faith again.

Satan wants us to develop bad memories as far as faith is concerned. He wants us to forget all that God has done so that we will doubt all that God can do. We need to keep alive the exercise of remembering in faith so that we can say, 'Thus far has the Lord led us'.

What do we do with our doubts then? Well, first of all I believe we will get ourselves into a knot if we try to deny that we have them. There are a few steps that I have found helpful.

1. Realise the nature of doubt

Some people react to doubt as though it were a mortal sin. Doubt, like temptation, is not sin. Unbelief is sin and if we remain too long in doubt we may find ourselves slipping into unbelief. We need to realise that doubt can be treated.

2. Recognise its value

Doubt can be seen as a sort of test. I believe the Lord uses doubt to sift out what is wrong in our thinking.

Often we come to such a pass that we can do nothing any longer to help ourselves. This is where God comes in and brings that word of strength that is needed for the hour. Faith that is not tested is not worth the name of faith. Faith that has been tested in the furnace of doubt will stand almost any other assault that man or Satan can throw at it.

3. Repent of known sin

Doubt does arise from sin, because we can't try to live a life of faith when something in that life contradicts the very basic element of faith which is trust. The Lord sometimes allows doubt to increase until we begin to realise that the root of it lies within our own life. The only thing we can do is turn away from that sin and look to the Father for forgiveness and restoration.

'If we confess our sins, he is faithful and just and will forgive us our sins and purify us from all unrighteousness' (1 John 1.9).

4. Receive the love of God

The greatest security in any life is love. The greatest security in the life of faith is the love of the Father made real within our own hearts. When we know the love of God, then nothing else in the whole world will be able to set us off course (see Romans 8. 31 and 39). In the same epistle Paul teaches us that this love is the outcome of the work of the Holy Spirit within our hearts:

'God has poured out his love into our hearts by the Holy Spirit, whom he has given us' (Romans 5.5).

What is important is that we don't become accustomed to living in doubt. Doubt undealt with becomes unbelief, and unbelief is the opposite of faith. Allow God to make it creative within your heart, grow through it into faith and see the tremendous fruit that the Father wants to bring in your life.

XIII

Enemy action

Faith operates under attack.

Earlier I spoke of the crucible principle of faith. Satan knows that he cannot attack the plan of God in a direct sense, so what he does is attack the crucible within which that purpose is placed.

We need to recognise that to choose a life of faith is to choose a life of warfare. In our hearts and lives God is at work bringing his purpose to fruition, so that it is our persons and lives that are especially the target for Satan and his opposition to the will of the Father.

I now take it for granted that, if we are involved in an important faith project, then we will begin to feel the attack of the enemy in a particularly strong and personal way. Satan is a dirty fighter and he leaves no avenue unexplored by which to achieve his devious ends.

One of the things that has moved me in recent days has been the number of people who have written to me or have said to me that they feel called to stand in prayer in a special way because of the particular ministry that God has given me. I confess that I often think other people see what

that ministry is more than I do, but I know that it has to do with faith. I believe that faith has become the most important issue for the Christian church today. Many do not recognise this at the moment and our interest is taken up with many different issues, some of which are highly activist and look very relevant to the needs of the hour. But I believe the greatest need of the hour is that God's people learn to live God's way on the principle of faith.

As far as I am concerned we live in the middle of open warfare and what is being challenged is the sovereign power and uniqueness of the God whom Jesus revealed. Jesus lived out the principle of faith and he is looking, I believe, for men and women who will bring that same principle into effect in these closing days of the twentieth century.

Such men and women will, however, need to be willing for the warfare that faith brings, because immediately they decide to trust God in an absolute sense they become prime targets for the onslaught of Satan and his agents.

Of course the Devil is not so stupid as to use overt means to achieve his ends. Men and women of faith would very soon suss that out and withstand it. What Satan does is to use other things, many of them legitimate in themselves, to gain his goal.

It is when that attack becomes personal that it is hard to live with. Yet if we give ourselves to be the crucibles of faith we need to ask how else it can be. We are the only targets that Satan has for attack.

Faith has, for me, become a way of life. I am not on the outside a very pious person and my friends will tell you that I am noted for calling a spade a spade, but I am passionately committed to the idea that God is all-powerful and that through faith he is able to achieve his will in this world. In fact, I don't believe there is any area of human experience that is outside his control. That is why, I believe, Jesus taught us to think of the Father/child image in relation to faith. The child has implicit trust in a loving Father and believes there is nothing he cannot do. So it is with faith. The child also knows implicitly that the Father knows best. So it is with faith.

Questions about why God does or does not answer prayer are not the most important for the man or woman of faith. They know the Father. They know that the Father always answers, and they know that the Father knows best and will answer in his way. They also know that if they take time to enquire before they ask, the Father will share with them his perfect will.

The Roffey Place enterprise has become, for me, the epitome of faith, but it is not on its own. The whole of life is faith and every day we minister from the Bethany Fellowship, we realise that without faith we could not continue the work.

I discover every new day carries with it a fresh challenge for faith. I also find that it carries with it another element of warfare. We stand against a restless enemy and that is why we need to be diligent in our alertness and readiness for action.

Satan uses anything he can find, or anything we will let him use, to try and attack us. Sometimes I feel it is like one army overrunning the defences of another. To begin with they fight with their own weapons, then when they have overrun part of the opposition's territory they will pick up their weapons and use them against their original owners. It's like that with us. Satan comes at us with things that are foreign to our experience to try and overwhelm us. Then he changes tactics and uses factors from within our own experience to destroy us from within.

Let me illustrate what I mean from personal experience.

Every time over the last two years that I have been involved in a major venture of faith I have soon found other things happening. One of the difficulties that I have found hardest to bear for myself and others close to me in the ministry has been outright attack on the nature of ministry and personal reputation. The Lord has shown us how to stand back from that without indulging in self-defence. Nevertheless, there are few things more hurtful to the spirit than to have slander and doubt poured over the good things that God has been doing in one's own life and work. Yet that is the way of Satan. He is seeking to demolish faith by way of personal discouragement. He knows well that faith works in crucibles and that, if he can destroy the crucible, faith will be lost.

Another area of attack has been physical illness. For the past two years or more, I have been dogged by a strange illness of the soft tissues. Suddenly, for no apparent reason, violent swelling of the face or of internal organs occurs which makes life almost unbearable. I have needed to learn to resist that progressively in prayer knowing that it is not the will of the Father, but the attack of the enemy. Satan can soon breed dejection and condemnation through such attacks.

These and many other things are the weapons of Satan to try and overcome the victory of faith. Of course, he knows and we need to learn that he is a defeated enemy and that ultimately all he can do is inflict flesh wounds that don't touch the spirit or destroy faith. However, he does resort to other methods as well.

Sometimes he will try and take advantage of things that find a legitimate place within one's own life. They are right to be there but Satan tries to bring evil out of them instead of good. For me, that has been in the area of emotions. For the last five years, I have had the privilege of having as the main support in my team a great friend called Katie. She became a Christian through my own ministry nine years ago while I was chaplain to her college in the University of Durham. We have shared many powerful times of ministry together and have learned many deep lessons of faith.

This year Katie became engaged to be married to Jeremy, another member of the Fellowship. Now, on the surface that was a great joy. It was something we have been praying about for years, but it happened at a most crucial time, just as Roffey Place was developing and I was feeling the cost of that faith enterprise. Satan then becomes the enemy within. He takes deep-seated feelings and emotions and turns them against faith. He does not concern himself with the devastation he causes, his one aim is to prevent faith being a live and active agent in the heart of the believer.

We need to understand the warfare of faith because if we don't we may be led into believing that faith is an easy option that delivers us from every difficulty and stress. The reverse is rather the case. Faith induces warfare because Satan sees a direct opportunity to thwart the purpose of the kingdom of God.

We need to learn also how to respond to this attack and how to turn Satan's tables on himself so that he is overthrown. I discovered certain principles through the ongoing intensity of this attack that I believe are fundamental to the battle of faith.

Firstly, it is important to learn to take the pain into yourself. If we try to avoid or deny the pain of personal attack, then we become reactive and negative and begin to lash out at those who attack us in such a way as to bring even more hurt upon ourselves. What Satan knows nothing about is suffering love. That is how Jesus defeated him on the cross. Jesus took the pain into himself and allowed the Father to redeem it. It helps to remember that, because none of us are called upon to suffer anything like the personal attack that Jesus underwent. Yet, 'When they hurled their insults at him, he did not retaliate' (1 Peter 2.23).

Pain that is not returned but taken before the throne of grace has tremendous redemptive power. I have seen situations, in which there seemed no possibility of restoration, brought to wholeness through the power of redemptive pain.

God can make pain very creative and, although we may need to wait his time, he can do far more with accepted pain than we can ever do by rejecting it.

Secondly, such attack leads us into a new reliance on the Father. If our heart is clear then we know that the Father knows us as well. He gives us the Spirit:

'The one who is in you is greater than the one who is in the world' (1 John 4.4).

I have found that the dual effect of such attack has often been that, on the one hand it has brought about a complete stripping down of myself, while on the other, it has developed a completely new reliance on God.

It's not a bad thing when we come to the end of ourselves. Often there are truths to be faced in this situation that otherwise would be unpalatable. God uses those moments to draw us closer to himself and to assure us of his love.

Thirdly, such personal attack leads to a complete re-assessment of life. When attack comes at the heart of your work and ministry or to some part of your character, then it leads you to question the whole reason and value of all that you are involved in.

It places a question mark against the directions that are being taken in ministry. It threatens the securities and relationships that have become important in life. In the end the attack can be so searching that we are left only with the Lord.

The thing to remember is that Satan always over-reaches himself. In attempting to destroy all these other elements of life, the last thing he intended was that we would discover the only ultimately important one, the reality and presence of God.

Of course, at the last, it is the very faith that the Devil is seeking to extinguish that is the secret of our victory. He wants us to leave our greatest weapon untried. He wants us to fight in the power of the flesh and human effort. He wants us to react to his attack in our own strength. But victory comes to those who choose to live by faith. Paul underlines this fact in his letter to the Ephesians:

'In addition to all this, take up the shield of faith, with which you can extinguish all the flaming arrows of the evil one' (Ephesians 6.16).

When faith is under attack, ask for more of it. It always has been a gift. It comes direct from the heart of the Father. It is his means of accomplishing his will through our lives. It is also his means of giving us the victory over every attack of the evil one. Through the power of the Holy Spirit who builds faith into our lives we discover the truth of John's words:

'The one who is in you is greater than the one who is in the world' (1 John 1.4).

XIV

Homing in

The Bible is a handbook of faith. That is why a life of faith demands that we take the Bible seriously. Much talk of trusting God today is vitiated by a weak view of Scripture. That is not only the fault of a liberal view that seeks to dilute the power of Scripture by human reason. It can be the fault of a conservative view that limits the power of God's word by a mechanical and stulted approach to the Bible. The Bible is a much more living mechanism of faith than most of us realise and for that reason we need to let it speak to us in a multitude of ways.

Our commitment to a total approach to Scripture for our study, paying attention to context and all the right questions, should in no way limit our approach to the Scripture for faith. Here the Spirit may open the Scripture up at a completely different level and seem to ignore what for us are paramount questions with regard to literature and history.

One of the great lessons that a life of faith soon teaches is that of the importance of Scripture in every dimension. The Scriptures centre on the person of faith par excellence: 'Jesus, the author and perfecter of our faith' (Hebrews 12.2). They show us the power of faith in action in the lives of countless men and women. The eleventh chapter of Hebrews is a compendium of what we can learn through the examples of faith set within Scriptures. The Bible is full of promises of faith on which we can depend and through which the Holy Spirit will stimulate and encourage us. It teaches us the principles of faith as we hear them from the lips of Jesus. Faith, for him, was the great principle of the kingdom of heaven.

Faith looks for an immediacy in Scripture that will lead and direct its steps. For faith the Scriptures become the voice of God as he speaks to those with ears to hear.

Some time ago, I flew from southern Sudan up the rift Valley into Kenya. We were in a small aircraft of the Missionary Aviation Fellowship and, due to some technical difficulties, had been delayed on our take-off. We had originally planned to fly all the way in daylight and land in Wilson field, the MAF home-base on the outskirts of Nairobi. By the time we got there it was very dark and we had to divert to Nairobi International airport where there were facilities for landing at night. It was an exciting experience because in that small plane we spent a long time skirting round a number of violent electric storms. It seemed as though we would never find our way in the dark, until suddenly in front of us we saw the landing lights of the airport.

We seemed so small, surrounded by the vastness of night and yet, when the lights came on, it was a whole new world. We knew where we were in relation to them and we knew where we were going because of them. With some relief and thanksgiving we landed the small plane right down the middle of the flight path usually reserved for international jumbo jets.

It is almost a rule of faith that when things seem their darkest, God is about to break forth with light. That was our experience with Roffey Place. It was at the times of most intense darkness that the Lord suddenly spoke with a clear guiding voice through the light of his word in Scripture. In fact, so true is this that we have taken those words of Psalm 119.130 as the motto for the college:

'The entrance of your words gives light'.

Many, many Scriptures came alive during the period of waiting in faith. Many folks in the fellowship began to sense the Holy Spirit speaking to them in new ways through Scripture. However, there were three words from Scripture that yielded great fruit in my experience. They were like the brightest lights of the flight path. The others were all important, but these were the bright shining signal lamps that kept us right on course throughout the venture. After they were first received I found myself going back to them time and again and would discover that they still spoke with that clarity and sharpness of the first hearing.

The first of these Scriptures was brought to me right at the outset of the venture by the brother who had first laid the brochure on my desk, Grahame Scofield. They were the words of Jeremiah 32.7:

'Buy my field at Anathoth, because as nearest relative it is your right and duty to buy it'.

We found ourselves back at this Scripture many times. It does not take a degree in biblical criticism to see that the geographical allusions in the text were not very pertinent to us. It is equally easy for the eye of faith to perceive that the spiritual principles of the text were. Of course, at the outset, it seemed like a straightforward direction from the Lord to go ahead and purchase the college – and so it was. But as time went on and we became aware of the part history of the place and how, for the past number of years, it had been re-furbished but hardly used, the whole notion of redemption took on a new meaning. It seemed that the Lord was saying that we would take this marvellous property and do with it something the world had been unable to do. What had proved to them to be a white elephant would become something to the glory of God. This is now happening.

Another important principle emerged under the impact of the text as to how we were to obtain it. I have already indicated how we considered taking out a mortgage or loan on the property to secure its purchase. The main stumbling-block to that whole idea was this verse of Scripture. It seemed to make clear that we had to purchase it in such a way that it would be unencumbered by debt, that it would be ours to possess. Of course, there was no thought of gain or self-interest in that idea. Rather it was the thought that the college should be free from any burden that might, in the end, determine the principles on which we acted with regard to its use.

As it happened, that is exactly what came to pass. We were able to buy the property without debt and with the complete freedom to found Roffey Place Christian Training Centre in the principles of faith which God has shown to us.

The second of these Scriptures comes from Deuteronomy chapter 28.3. This is the promise of the Lord through Moses to Joshua just before the children of Israel enter the land of promise:

'You will be blessed in the city and blessed in the country'.

I have already spoken in chapter 3 of the power of this word and how appropriate it was within the life of the fellowship. The fact that we had just completed purchase of an old cinema in the middle of Brighton was enough, but the fact that the name The City had been chosen for the new outreach centre to be based there was another pointer to faith.

This Scripture was given to me from more than one source within the Bethany Fellowship. It was a Scripture that I had been given in my reading one morning and it seemed to come alight from the page. So much so that I preached on it one Sunday morning during our worship at The Hyde. I felt personally that it was a strong indication of the rightness of Roffey Place as a particular set of buildings since they are strategically placed just between Crawley and Horsham, in the country.

It was, however, none of these particular witnesses that brought the Scripture home to me ultimately. It was the fact that just at one of the darkest moments of our waiting, David Brown, the elder who leads the work at Abbots Leigh and the City, came over to support me one night in a prayer meeting at The Hyde. Every other elder was away on holiday and there were relatively few people left at that time in the fellowship. Imagine my surprise when he came to me with the words of Deuteronomy chapter 28.3 which someone in a completely separate part of the Fellowship life had received for me as a promise from the Lord. It was in the mouth of two or three witnesses!

The third of these Scriptures came to me first of all through Hilda, my wife. It was the words of Isaiah 66.9:

"'Do I bring to the moment of birth and not give delivery?" says the Lord. "Do I close up the womb when I bring to delivery?" says your God'.

The interesting fact about some of these Scriptures was their persistence. This particular scripture was given fairly early on in the proceedings and we took it as a very clear word of encouragement that God would provide the means to complete what had been started. In fact this word was first given to us right at the time when we were due to put the deposit on the place and it provided a great stimulus for faith to move ahead. On that and many other grounds we moved forward by placing the deposit thus moving into the next stage of the action.

But the Lord was not finished with this witness yet. In the very final days, when we felt the real pressure and tension of faith it was these words that he brought back powerfully to our remembrance. I can remember sitting in my study with a few friends. We met to pray about the situation which had become very final indeed. In the middle of that time, these words sprang to life again, like a voice from the dead. It was, for me, as though the Lord had announced them directly into the room. I felt a great sense of anticipation and peace, feeling that we had received the last word on the subject. At that moment we had no idea how it was going to be fulfilled and the pregnancy seemed just a little overdue! But the following day we found out via the phone call from Colin and we were able to praise God for the faithfulness of his word.

There were, of course, many other words, but I share these to illustrate just how apposite the witness of Scripture can be to a situation of faith in our own modern day. It sometimes feels, in a situation like this, as though the Holy Spirit has prepared the words specially for us, but then maybe he has!

There is, I believe, a prophetic element in this use of Scripture, or maybe it would be better to say that in this kind of situation Scripture comes to us prophetically, because it is not the outcome of systematic consideration of Scripture. Indeed, on occasions like this Scripture will be released into our lives from parts of the Bible we seem never to have read before or in ways that are different from normal methods of Bible study, sometimes in a daily reading aid like *The Daily Light*.

Of course, we need to be careful about this approach to the Bible. The only case I would make is that it is not an approach to the Bible, it is more the Bible's approach to us. It comes at us with surprise, unexpectedly and with power and relevance that is often missing in the normal run of our regular Bible study. This in no way denies that the same can happen through more regular means or, indeed, that those are essential for our growth in the Christian life. It merely affirms what faith already knows, that the Holy Spirit is not limited to our mechanical approaches to the Scripture for him to unleash the word of God into our lives.

I believe it is prophetic because certain simple ground rules have become apparent in my experience of Scripture in this way. These ground rules are very close to those which I would associate with the function of prophecy. They are these:

First, *a sense of given-ness*. There is something utterly fresh and spontaneous about such a release of Scripture. It does not follow the normal rules of biblical mining. Whenever we begin to try and engineer such words they no longer carry with them that freshness and power that is the hallmark of prophetic Scripture.

It is interesting to note that once Scripture has been received in this way two or three times with obvious effect, others will begin to try and copy the same effect with other Scriptures. It may be that these have a certain value but they will not have that ring of truth about them which the first Scriptures had. In fact, this is one way you

can be sure that God is speaking. We found it necessary to go back time and again to the first important words that guided our faith. It was not difficult to discern what
they were because they stood out like bright stars on a dark night.

Second, *a sense of immediacy and relevance*. I am staggered sometimes at the appropriateness of the Scriptures which the Holy Spirit brings. Often I have to confess to never having consciously noticed them before. That, for me, is another hallmark of truth. These Scriptures come to us like stumbled-upon pearls. I will never forget the joy of my surprise some years ago when Hilda and I were about to leave Durham where I had been the minister of a church for eight years. We had no idea where the path was going to lead. One other person was going with us to help in the work, a single woman in her mid-twenties whom we knew well. I just wanted some simple confirmation that it was right.

I opened my Bible and there in front of my eyes were the words of Jeremiah 3.14:

'I will choose one of you from every town and two
from every clan and bring you to Zion'.

Here I was, a Scotsman, reading about clans in the Old Testament!

Prophetic words have immediate reference. Mind you, they may not immediately come to pass, but they will be speaking directly and immediately into the situation in hand.

Third, *a sense of purpose*. One of the things that annoys me most about so called words of prophecy today is that they call for nothing. Prophecy calls for response. It is a word from the Lord that carries direction or warning or promise within it. It is not just a bland thought of encouragement. If it is a word of promise then there is preparation for the promise, if it is warning then there is repentance for the sin, if it is direction then there is obedience in action. But God's words in these situations are action words. They prevent, help or direct action on the part of God's people.

Faith believes that God is a speaking God. He has an opinion about everything and a purpose for his people. His desire is to share that purpose with us so that we can share in it with him.

To this end he brings us his living word in the power of the Holy Spirit. He speaks with a voice of authority and with a word of power:

> "'For my thoughts are not your thoughts, neither are your ways my ways", declares the Lord ". . . As the rain and the snow come down from heaven, and do not return to it without watering the earth and making it bud and flourish, so that it yields seed for the sower and bread for the eater, so is my word that goes out from my mouth: it will not return to me empty, but will accomplish what I desire and achieve the purpose for which I sent it'" (Isaiah 55.8-11).

XV

Handbook of faith

The Scriptures challenge a narrow view of faith. Faith, for many people amounts to little more than claiming the promises of Jesus in Scripture and an expectancy that these things will become real for them in their experience. That is good. Such faith has been at a discount in the church at large and I believe that the Father today is looking for men and women who will trust what he has promised in Jesus and live on the strength of that. All the promises of God, as Paul told the Corinthians, are yes and amen in him (2 Corinthians 1.20).

But there is more to faith than that and it is as we look at the teaching of Scripture that we are able to perceive this truth. Faith, for the New Testament, is a multi-coloured thing. It operates at a number of different and yet closely related levels. Faith is presented to us rather like the floors of a multi-storey building. There is no good trying to build the top floor first. The foundations have got to be right so that what is built is sound and can bear great strain. Living by faith is bearing the load. It means taking the strain, and if our foundations are not strong then we will soon collapse under that load.

This is why when a person is brought to living faith through the work of the Holy Spirit their eyes soon turn in the direction of Scripture. I always watch with joy this movement in the life of new Christians. It is a hallmark of the reality and depth of the work of Christ in their lives that they begin to see what the Scriptures have to say about every aspect of their experience. One of the great dangers of the contemporary renewal movement in certain parts of the traditional church is that it has never been allowed to come under the authority of Scripture. But faith is created and faith is informed by the living word of God, and while it is true, especially in the lives of people who have been far outside the Christian fold, that God speaks powerfully in other ways, there is no clearer expression of the word of God than Scripture. The Holy Spirit has laid the deposit of truth there so that we might be guided into right thinking and so that our lives might be moulded into right living.

The more we are determined to live the faith life, the more we will discover that we cannot do it apart from the written word of God.

There are at least three important levels of faith presented to us through Scripture of which we must be aware. These are the three main storeys in the Holy Spirit's building of faith in our lives.

First, there is that dimension of faith of which Paul speaks in *1 Corinthians 16.13:*

'Be on your guard; stand firm in **the** faith; be men of courage; be strong'.

This way of speaking of faith is echoed in the short letter of Jude and verse 3:

'Dear friends, although I was very eager to write to you about the salvation we share, I felt I had to write and urge you to contend for **the** *faith that was once for all entrusted to the saints'*.

The very style of the language and the use of the definite article in front of the word 'faith' tells us something important. Here, the writers are not only speaking of an experience of faith or of claiming the promises of faith in Scripture. Here they are speaking of something that is recognized amongst believers as a *deposit of truth*.

We need to understand that this is where faith takes its strength from. It is not only important *that* we believe, it is important *what* we believe and *in whom* we believe.

Jesus declared that the work of the Holy Spirit would be to lead his followers into the truth concerning himself:

'When he, the Spirit of truth, comes, he will guide you into all truth. He will not speak on his own; he will speak only what he hears, and he will tell you what is yet to come. He will bring glory to me by taking from what is mine and making it known to you' (John 16.13–14).

I have never yet met a person who was filled with the Holy Spirit who was a heretic concerning the person and work of Jesus. When he writes to the Corinthians, Paul makes it clear that the first important move of the Holy Spirit within our hearts is to bring us to a proper confession concerning Jesus:

'Therefore I tell you that no-one who is speaking by the Spirit of God says, "Jesus be cursed," and no-one can say, "Jesus is Lord," except by the Holy Spirit'.

Faith depends on a right view of God. The Holy Spirit, who, of course, is God, expounds the Father and the Son into our hearts. It is by the Spirit that we cry, *Abba*, Father' (Romans 8.15) and it is by the Spirit that we have a true relationship with the Son (Romans 10.9).

I was brought up with a race of Christian men who were not easily fooled when it came to this dimension of faith. Like the rest of us they had their faults, but they knew their Bibles. The result was that they knew God. They had a high view of his authority and sovereignty. They knew the truth within their hearts and they had an awesome capacity to discern heresy.

Of course that way of thinking is not popular in much of the Church today. We have become soft as far as truth is concerned. We have abdicated the great essential verities and have been consumed in our interests with piffling side issues that have little to do with the heart of faith.

Faith centres in the great things of God. It sees his vitality, it is aware of his majesty, it bows before his holiness, it trusts his love, it depends on his power, it emulates his character. That is why 'without faith it is impossible to please God' (Hebrews 11.6).

The Holy Spirit's concern is first to bring us into **the faith**. When we know who God really is and what he is capable of, then we know where to put our trust. Today the Church argues about form and liturgy, about ceremonial and ecclesiastical details and all the while it allows people to operate with every warped view of God or none at all. That is why living faith is so desperately missing from many of our Church councils and leaders' meetings. It is not because of the absence of promises: it is because of the absence of premises. If the foundations are not right, then faith cannot function. Faith cannot be a living reality apart from a living God. Faith centres in on the reality of God who by his living power raised Jesus from the dead. That is precisely the point Paul is making in 1 Corinthians chapter 15:

'And if Christ has not been raised, our preaching is useless *and so is your faith*' *(verse 14)*.

Such a foundation is vital. Today it is popular to modify even such an important truth as the resurrection of Jesus from the dead, and yet this is probably the most important element of **the faith,** because faith depends on the ability of God to act in power. Where more did he act in power than in the resurrection of Jesus from the dead?

This kind of truth has nothing at all to do with peripheral questions of church form and order of ministry. In fact, most of these had never been invented in New Testament times. It has to do with the heart of God. It has to do with a right conception of God and his work for us in Jesus. It is on Jesus and our view of him that faith depends from first to last.

Let's see the necessity therefore, if we want to live by faith, of opening our hearts and minds up to the revelation of Scripture. The Christian has been led into freedom by the work of the Holy Spirit, but, as Paul showed the Galatians, it is not the freedom to please ourselves in relation to our ideas about God. It is freedom from the power and thraldom of sin, precisely because we have been brought into a proper view of God in Christ by the living work of the Spirit in our hearts. This lays an obligation upon us to remain open to the revelation of the word of God in Scripture. There we will discover the true foundation for our faith day by day and the more we come to know the Father through his word, the more our faith will be founded on sure ground and the stronger our faith will become.

Then, however, Scripture moves us on from that foundation to another level of faith. It is easy to see why this is so because there is always the danger that *what* we believe about God will petrify and become a dead system of doctrine. That is the case in most denominations today. They all have a confession of faith that stands more or less in line with the historic creeds of the Church. Yet within the ranks, even of the clergy of these denominations, are men and women who would give no allegiance to these historic confessions. How can this be? It is because doctrine has become stultified. What used to have life is now dead, and people can never be moved or controlled by something that is a dead letter. The only real control of truth is the vital, living witness of the Holy Spirit within our hearts and in our midst.

So the *second* level of faith that Scripture demonstrates for us is that *faith without deeds is dead.* Just as the first level of faith has to do with *what* we believe, *the truth of Jesus expounded into our hearts by the Spirit*, so this second level has to do with *how* we believe. That is, faith is not a static thing but an active reality in our lives: *it is the works of Jesus manifested in our lives by the Holy Spirit.*

It is the short epistle of James, that spells this out so clearly. Luther described the epistle of James as 'a right strawy epistle'. He was so keen on the idea of 'justification by faith' which he discovered in the Pauline epistles that he thought that James was contradicting this. So he wanted to excise the letter of James from the Christian canon of scripture. He was wrong.

No idea is so dynamic for our daily living than that faith should be active. This is no contradiction to the fact that we are justified by faith. In fact, it ought to be the outcome of it.

What the Father wants to see in our lives today is a manifestation of the power of the kingdom of God through works of faith. I believe that there is nothing so powerful in terms of witness to non-Christians than faith at work in action.

Now we need to be clear what we mean by this. What I don't mean are those efforts with which the church is riddled in the name of humanitarianism and self-effort. The symbol of faith-in-absence for many churches is a barometer on a board proclaiming to the world at large just how much of a deficit of belief that congregation has for the provision of God. The fact that church life is littered with the stupidity of jumble sales and autumn fairs is only another sign that it has chosen to try and support the work of the kingdom by the same means the

world runs its bazaars and clubs. It is a travesty of the kingdom of heaven.

What the world needs to see today is the real thing. It requires a living demonstration that the claims we make for faith are true. Of course, perhaps this is why so few claims are made for faith in the church at large, because in our own lives and congregations we don't know if they are true for ourselves.

Jesus himself made it clear that it was his intention that our lives should be showplaces of the works of faith:

'I tell you the truth, anyone who has faith in me will do what I have been doing. He will do even greater things than these, because I am going to the Father' (John 14.12).

This is one of those difficult words of Jesus. What on earth could he have meant? He meant, I believe, what he said: because he was rising in ascended power to the Father, he would be able to operate in that unlimited power in the lives of countless believers who would put their faith in him.

Living faith needs to find its expression in our deeds. This is where the demand of faith begins, because we need to recognise the fact that the cost of such faith may very well begin within our own lives. If we are going to ask the Lord to meet the needs of those around us, then we need to be willing to understand that he asks that the first part of the answer come from our own lives.

Jesus himself used this active dimension of faith as the absolute proof of the presence of the kingdom of God:

> 'If I drive out demons by the Spirit of God (the older Authorised version gives a literal translation: 'the finger of God') then the kingdom of God has come upon you' (Matthew 12.28).

The idea of the finger of God is a living metaphor from the Old Testament. God's finger leaves its mark. The traces of his work are there for all to see. It was the finger of God that wrote the law on Sinai. It was the finger of God that appeared on the wall of Belshazzar's banqueting hall. Men need to see the finger of God in our lives through faith in action in the name of Jesus. The most powerful evangelistic witness today will not be more words of exposition. We need words of explanation. That is what happened on the day of Pentecost. Peter's great evangelistic sermon was in reality an explanation of the events that were taking place before the very eyes of the onlookers.

> 'These men are not drunk, as you suppose. It's only nine in the morning! No, this is what was spoken by the prophet Joel: "In the last days, God says, I will pour out my Spirit on all people"'(Acts 2.15–16).

The third element of faith in the New Testament grows directly out of these two, becuase the one undeniable fact about the Scriptures is that they are chock full of promises. The Father has not only provided us with the grounds for faith, by showing us something about himself through Scripture, nor has he only shown us the power for faith and promised us that through the Holy Spirit within, but he has provided rich promises with which faith can operate.

The Gospels themselves rule with promises of faith, words which are not only an encouragement to faith but which are the active tools with which faith works. These words of promise breathe life, they carry within themselves by the power of the Spirit, the means to become reality in the life of the believer. They urge us to put faith into action, but they themselves become the means of us putting faith into action.

I have already described the first two levels of faith as:

    1) *The truth of Jesus expounded into our hearts by the Holy Spirit*;

and 2) *The works of Jesus manifested in our lives by the Holy Spirit*.

It would be right to describe this third level of faith as:

    3) *The promises of the word of God made real in our experience by the Holy Spirit.*

What the Spirit does is to lift the words of promise off the page and plant them in our hearts as living words that make faith active within us. These words are of great variety within the Scripture. As I demonstrated in the last chapter, they are often words of direct guidance that lead us into certain steps of faith. At other times they are powerful words that bring faith to life. The words of Jesus are specially important here:

'You may ask me for anything in my name, and I will do it' (John 14.14).

'Ask and it will be given to you; seek and you will find; knock and the door will be opened to you. For everyone who asks receives; he who seeks finds, and to him who knocks, the door will be opened' (Luke 11.9–10).

'I tell you that if two of you on earth agree about anything you ask for, it will be done for you by my Father in heaven. For where two or three come together in my name, there am I with them' (Matthew 18.19–20).

Those people who spend their time speculating on the truth of such promises should spend less time discussing the problem and more putting the promise into action. As the old dictum says, 'The proof of the pudding is in the eating'.

I have discovered many times in my life, and we certainly found this to be true during the Roffey Place enterprise, that these simple promises actually contain many of the deep principles of faith.

So when we say that the Bible is a handbook of faith, we don't mean that it merely contains a series of proof texts to which we can lay claim for every situation, but something much more than that. The Scriptures educate us with regard to the true nature of faith. Through the Scriptures we can begin to see the full dimensions of faith so that we gain encouragement and foundation for our ongoing trust in God the Father. This is why the great leaders of the Reformation in Europe took their stand on these two important pillars: 'SOLA SCRIPTURA, SOLA FIDES': 'Scripture alone, faith alone'. They knew that the two went hand in hand and the one grew out of and into the other.

XVI

Fit for faith

There is yet another way in which Scripture is important to the life of faith. This is through the effect it has in moulding my own life and bringing about that change which is so necessary if my life and character are to be fit for faith.

There are close parallels between physical and spiritual fitness. If an athlete or player is going to meet the demands of his calling, then his body has to be kept in trim so that it can fulfil the requirements of the sport. There would be little point or future in a footballer taking the field, if his body was not in a condition that made him able to play the game. He might know all the tactics and technical secrets of the profession but they would be mere theory without that correlative fitness of his body to put them into action.

So it is in the realm of the Spirit. I believe that the greatest hindrance to faith being an active reality in the lives of many Christians is the simple fact that their lives are not in that state of preparation to meet the demands of faith.

Just as the athlete has certain routine exercises for fitness which are appropriate to his sport, so the Christian has regular spiritual fitness exercises which direct him into the right ways and means of preparation for the rigours of faith. I know from my own experience, for example that the greatest threat to a life of faith is not my lack of understanding of Biblical promises or anything like that, it is sin. Sin is moral weakness, it is a flaw of character that brings a cloud into that open relationship which faith requires between God the Father and my own spirit.

Sin takes many forms in my life. It does not only mean those overt actions of wrong deeds or attitudes. It goes much deeper than that. Sin breeds in the interior darkness of one's spirit and issues in coldness of heart or unbelief in relation to the things of faith. Sin can be that wrong tiredness into which we easily slip when we pay too little attention to the Maker's instructions for our minds and bodies. The Devil looks for those things within each of our personalities upon which he can play so that we move out of the fitness of faith into weakness and inadequacy. Being spiritually out-of-sorts is the death-knell of active belief.

It is here that Scripture is so important to vital faith. I have discovered through experiences, like standing in faith for Roffey Place, the powerful need to let the word of God in Scripture have its place within my own life. The writer of Psalm 119 made the very same discovery with regard to God's word in his life:

'How can a young man keep his way pure? By living according to your word. I seek you with all my heart; do not let me stray from your command' (Psalm 119.9–10).

As the pressure of faith builds up I have found myself time and again wrestling with reactions in my mind and other thoughts that are not at all related to the main items on the faith agenda. I would say that if we are going to live by faith then we need to learn to expect that many other parts of our lives will be stirred up, almost, at times, into a ferment, because through this Satan is seeking to overthrow the work of faith that God wants to do in our lives.

This is where continual openness to the word of God in Scripture is so important.

It is important *firstly*, I believe, because it is through Scripture that we experience the difference between the condemnation of Satan and *the conviction of the Holy Spirit*. There are no doubt things that are wrong within our experience. What Satan wants to do is find these things and play on them so that they lead to still more wrong. What the Father wants to do is gently to expose them in truth so that they can be dealt with and taken out of the way so that faith can breathe. That is called conviction. The writer to the Hebrews makes it clear when he says:

> 'The word of God is living and active. Sharper than any double-edged sword, it penetrates even to dividing soul and spirit, joints and marrow; it judges the thoughts and attitudes of the heart. Nothing in all creation is hidden from God's sight. Everything is uncovered and laid bare before the eyes of him to whom we must give account' (Hebrews 4.12–13).

When I was a boy, there was one text of Scripture that was popular as a hanging text on walls. It frequently used to be framed in wood and stitched with embroidery. The words seemed very awesome to me at that time. They read: 'THOU GOD SEEST ME'. I have grown to love those words, because now I realise they are not words of condemnation but of conviction and assurance. The Psalmist knew that very real experience of God in his life when he wrote:

> 'O Lord, you have searched me and you know me.
> You know when I sit and when I rise,
> you perceive my thoughts from afar.
> You discern my going out and my lying down;
> you are familiar with all my ways.
> Before a word is on my tongue
> You know it completely, O Lord (Psalm 139. 1–4).

Now such an experience of God can either be a tremendous threat or a great comfort. The Psalmist knew it as the latter for he went on in his writing:

> 'How precious to me are your thoughts, O God!
> How vast is the sum of them!
> Were I to count them,
> they would outnumber the grains of sand,
> When I awake, I am still with you' (Psalm 139. 17–18).

'Search me, O God, and know my heart;
test me and know my anxious thoughts.
See if there is any offensive way in me,
and lead me in the way everlasting' (Psalm 139. 23–
24).

You see the Psalmist had discovered the value of the
convicting power of God in his life. He knew the need
and the security of allowing God to search his inmost
being and of allowing confession to flow into repentance and of repentance resulting in forgiveness and
healing.

This experience of the forgiveness and the love of God
is the ground of faith. When we have experienced for
ourselves the mighty power of God's forgiveness in our
lives, then we find it easy to believe that the same Father
is willing and able to answer all other prayers.

Secondly, it is through Scripture that we experience *the
power of God's word in the renewal of our minds*.

The mind is the inner stronghold of human experience. Whatever controls our minds will affect our
actions. That is why Satan attacks our minds. That is
why he so often tries to destroy us in the realm of our
imagination. Imagination is a very powerful factor within
our experience. A great part of our living takes place at
the level of our imagination. A great part of our *real*
experience is imaginary rather than actual. I say *real*
experience because many people act as though what takes
place in our imagination is not real. The real, for them, is
on the outside. What happens on the outside is very often
far from real. If we could let the real out then it would
become a re-play of those things which control our
imaginations.

Our minds are like blotting paper and they will absorb
what we choose to allow into them. If we want to live by
faith we need to recognise the importance of this area of
our experience and we need to understand the power of
God's word to cleanse our minds.

This is exactly what Paul means when he writes in
Romans 12.2:

'Do not conform any longer to the pattern of this world, but be transformed by the renewing of your mind. Then you will be able to test and approve what God's will is – his good, pleasing, and perfect will'.

Now the way that Satan will prevent the power of Scripture having this effect within our minds is by trying to prevent us from meditating upon the word. He will work on our imaginations to such an extent that we are in no fit state to sit quietly and meditate on the word of God or he will see to it that we are so busy we don't have time to. We need to be determined to resist all these ploys of the evil one and bring ourselves into those positions where we can take time to concentrate on the word of God.

'Blessed is the man
who does not walk in the counsel of the wicked
or stand in the way of sinners
or sit in the seat of mockers.
But his delight is in the law of the Lord,
and on his law he meditates day and night.
He is like a tree planted by streams of water,
which yields its fruit in season
and whose leaf does not wither.
Whatever he does prospers' (Psalm 1. 1–3).

Faith demands that we sit with God, that we discover the discipline of allowing the word of God into our minds and that God's word is allowed to sift through us and cleanse us from evil thoughts. Through the power of the word of God in our mind, the negative things of unbelief and darkness are supplanted by the powerful promises of God's kingdom. The control centre of our being is wrested from the domination of Satan and taken over in the power of the Holy Spirit to become fruitful in faith.

Thirdly, it is through the Scripture we experience the *assurance of God's word in our hearts*. I soon found out through a faith experience like Roffey Place that I became increasingly aware of my own inadequacy. There was a good side to this because it continually threw me back on to God. The Holy Spirit took me time and again back into the Scriptures and there I discovered the great assurances of faith and power in words like 2 Peter 1. 3– 4:

'His divine power has given us everything we need for life and godliness through our knowledge of him who called us by his own glory and goodness. Through these he has given us his very great and precious promises, so that through them you may participate in the divine nature and escape the corruption in the world caused by evil desires'.

At times when the inner battle has been particularly fierce, it has only been the reality of words like these that have prevented the desires becoming actions. You see what I have discovered about the Scriptures in situations like these is that they are so clear. Here, for example, in 1 Peter we have an unequivocal statement of faith. It leaves me in no doubt that God has made all that is required for a life of faith and holiness available to me through the power of the Holy Spirit. The result of this is that I am left in a situation of choice, whether to accept and act on the power of the word of God or whether to remain in unbelief and fall into sin. It is like a fitness chart for the athlete. Do this or eat this and you will not be able to stay the course. On the other hand, accept this diet or exercise and you will find you are able to achieve targets beyond your own imagination.

Faith soon learns that what the Scriptures say is true. They are not merely statements of information. They are the living, active word of God and if we will take them into our hearts they will become effective within our experience. The Scripture that tells us that God's power is available, if received in faith, will make that very power real within our lives.

Fourthly, of course, Scripture presents us with the great *examples of faith*. These come to us both as an encouragement and a challenge. We begin to see the men and women of faith, warts and all. We feel our hearts stirring within us to come to know such exploits of faith within our own lives. Hebrews chapter 11 encapsulates almost every great Biblical example of faith in one sweep. It drives us on in faith. It sets a target and teaches us how to get there in the power of Christ. It does not, in the end, leave us with men at all but drives us through to Jesus, 'the author and perfecter of our faith' (Hebrews 12.2).

Through the Scriptures, we are given something to fix our eyes on and to aim at in faith. To live by faith is to be part of a great tradition; it is to participate in a great heritage. The line runs from Abraham, the great father of the faithful, right through to our present lives. What a thought! It proceeds from the beginning of time right through to eternity. Faith takes its vision from a great perspective. When we live in the light of Scripture we can see that our faith is no local or merely personal affair. We are standing in that great line of men and women of God who are witnesses to the very faith in which we stand.

The twelfth chapter of Hebrews spells it out in a majestic, heart-stirring way:

'You have come to Mount Zion, to the heavenly Jerusalem, the city of the living God. You have come to thousands upon thousands of angels in joyful assembly, to the church of the firstborn, whose names are written in heaven. You have come to God, the judge of all men, to the spirits of righteous men made perfect, to Jesus the mediator of a new covenant, and to the sprinkled blood that speaks a better word than the blood of Abel' (Hebrews 12. 22–24).

That is the life-blood of faith! Satan wants to keep us house-bound, locked in the prison of our own small minds and evil thoughts. God wants to release us from all these things to share his visions of glory. For this reason he has given us the Scripture:

'For everything that was written in the past was written to teach us, so that through endurance and the encouragement of the Scriptures we might have hope' (Romans 15.4).

XVII

Leader of the opposition

I believe that is is very important that we stick closely to the revelation of Scripture as we seek to follow the Lord in faith. There are many reasons for this but one of the chief reasons is that we are in danger of being led up a great number of blind alleys today by thinking which bears little relationship to the revealed truth of God's word.

It is always the case during a war that the enemy seeks to foil the effectiveness of the campaign being waged against him by spreading false information and rumour which, if believed, would lead the people in wrong directions. I am told, by those who remember, that a favourite trick during the Second World War was simply to turn all the road signs in the opposite direction so that any invading force would be sent the wrong way and be led into total confusion. We all know when we are driving along country lanes how easy it is to lose course simply by the lack of a clear signpost at a crucial junction.

I firmly believe today that Satan is attempting within Christian circles to put up diversions and to spread rumours that are meant to lead God's people wildly astray. Many of these rumours are of the nature of exaggeration giving himself importance and power in the lives of men and women that the Scriptures deny him. Now don't get me wrong, I am by no means suggesting that Satan is not a real force to be reckoned with or that he cannot deal devastation into the lives of people. Anyone who takes the New Testament seriously cannot but believe that. He is described by Paul in Ephesians chapter 2 as 'the ruler of the kingdom of the air' (verse 2).

But we also need to remember Jesus' description of Satan: 'He is a liar and the father of lies' (John 8.44). We need to be very cautious in accepting any description of the power and work of Satan that comes from any source apart from the revelation of Scripture. Where our experience tallies with the teaching of Scripture well and good, but where elements are introduced that carry with them a strong degree of fanciful detail then we need to be careful that we are not being duped by an enemy plant, a piece of false information to lead us astray.

It seems to me that we suffer from two extremes in the Church today as far as Satan is concerned. First, we suffer from the *Devil-denying brigade*. Their philosophy is that Satan is the product of a first century world view and that all that Jesus was doing was employing the figurative language of his day to explain some of the more drastic realities of the human situation. In a nutshell, Satan does not exist and there is no such personification of evil. Second, we suffer from the *Devil-watching brigade* who see Satan round every corner and a demon under every bed. I don't doubt they are sincere and that their belief comes from very real awareness of the actual power of Satan that has grown out of a very real experience of the Holy Spirit, but it is truth exaggerated. The danger is that unwittingly we will give the Devil far more room than he deserves in our own and other people's experience and that we will be wasting our time demon-hunting when we should be proclaiming and standing in the completed victory of Jesus. It is always noticeable in the Scriptures that when Jesus or his true representatives arrived on the scene there is no longer trouble with demons. After all they are only agencies under authority. Their leader, Satan, has done such a good job in bringing them under his authority that when an even higher authority in spiritual terms arrives on the scene they have no difficulty recognising him. They not only recognise him but they submit to him and flee his presence. The outstanding example of this of course, is a story like that of the man amongst the tombs in Gadara who was possessed by so many demons that they said their name was Legion. When Jesus came, Legion went and inhabited the pigs and drove them over the cliff into the sea. Jesus never had a counselling session with demons; he addressed them and banished them so that they troubled the people no more.

Now I believe the secret of Jesus with regard to demons was his attitude towards Satan. Luke 4 makes it clear that he did not take Satan lightly. He regarded him as an evil and powerful and actual foe, but he also regarded him as someone who had already been put in his place under the authority of the word of God. This is something we do well to remember today. The New Testament does not teach dualism as far as God and the Devil are concerned. The Bible regards Satan as active in a limited zone under the permissive will of God and under final judgement, having been defeated once and for all in the victory of the Cross. In his death and resurrection Jesus has dealt the death-knell to every force of evil and it is in this victory that the Christian can stand:

'Having disarmed the powers and authorities, he made a public spectacle of them, triumphing over them by the cross' (Colossians 2.15).

This leads to a number of conclusions as far as I am concerned. During the time of standing in faith for Roffey Place, and indeed, in the months that have gone since, then, I have had to do great battle against the attacks of Satan. I have no doubt as to the reality and the ferocity of this and I have no doubt that his intention has been to try and destroy me physically and spiritually or both. The New Testament makes it clear that this is his intention:

'Your enemy the devil prowls around like a roaring lion looking for someone to devour' (1 Peter 5.8).

That is not a piece of first century speculation: this will be the first-hand experience of anyone who seeks to stand in faith. If Satan can have his way in our lives and bring us down, then he will effectively have destroyed the purpose of faith that God wanted to achieve through us. Therefore we need to be on our guard.

The very fact of spiritual attack however has led me to ask deep questions about the nature of this attack and the means of it within a Christian's experience. For the moment I am not concerned with the activities of Satan on the outside, that is amongst people who have never opened their lives to the Holy Spirit. I am sure that the evidence today points to the fact that the New Testament is again absolutely right when it says that 'the god of this age has blinded the minds of unbelievers, so that they cannot see the light of the gospel of the glory of Christ, who is the image of God' (2 Corinthians 4.4). Satan's interest is to prevent men and women from ever opening their minds to the truth of the gospel and entering the joy of the kingdom of light, but even here he overplays his hand. He may be devious but he is not the best master of strategy because time and again he overstates his case to such an extent that it becomes obvious to all what is afoot.

Jesus said, when he spoke of the activity of Satan, that 'when he lies, *he speaks his native language*, for he is a liar and the father of lies' (John 8.44). My own conviction is that even many of those people who worship Satan are being deluded by him. He has spun yarns into their hearts and minds with regard to his power and authority that the Scripture would never warrant. He has presented a public image of himself that in itself is a blind to the truth. We almost, at one level, operate with a benevolent idea of Satan as an old man with horns and a tail, a graphic opposite to our equally pathetic view of angels. The power of spiritual evil is much more subtle than this and I believe that Satan hardly ever discloses himself personally. Perhaps this is one of the chief reasons that the liberal church has become such an unbeliever in the personality of Satan. They have left the sure ground of Scripture and they have, therefore, no clear idea of what Satan is like. Their images of him are non-personal because they have never overtly met him within their own experience. So now they think that he is extinct, if he ever did exist at all. That is a master stroke on the part of Satan because the less conscious many people are about him, the more power he can wield within their lives by many other subtle means and subterfuges.

The New Testament makes the reality of spiritual evil very clear. It is interesting to notice as you read the Bible that there are only rare occasions when Satan is said to carry out his dirty work himself. The outstanding example of this is in the experience of Judas Iscariot when we are told that Satan dealt directly with him:

> 'Then Satan entered Judas, called Iscariot, one of the Twelve' (Luke 22.3).

In the Gospels and Acts we have many instances of people being possessed by or attacked by demons. Ephesians 6.12 also speaks of different levels of spiritual forces of evil: rulers, authorities, powers of this dark world, and spiritual forces in the heavenly realms. I believe that this description describes a real order of spiritual powers, all of which are set on thwarting the purposes of God and bringing men and women into bondage.

We need to be clear, however, what we are saying. I find it impossible to believe that a Christian who is open to the indwelling of the Holy Spirit and knows the life of Christ within them can be said to be *possessed* by Satan or demons. The witness of Scripture is that demonic powers are totally allergic to the presence of the Holy Spirit. It is often the case when the Holy Spirit begins to work in the lives of certain people who have been exposed to profound spiritual evil that exorcism of demons needs to take place over a period of time and in a progressive sense. This, it seems to me, is the forerunner of that person coming into the fullness of new birth and the complete recognition of Jesus as their Lord. Quite often this period of ministry will be violent and the battle will rage savagely between the powers of darkness and the Holy Spirit as they try to maintain their control in the individual's experience. Great anointings of faith are called for on the part of those who minister, not only against the possession but against fear and harm that threatens those who minister.

In our experience in the Fellowship this battle has sometimes culminated in a final fierce conflict perhaps with one or two last demon powers trying to make a last ditch stand against the Lordship of Jesus. At this moment there is need for great faith and strength through the Holy Spirit because Satan will stop at nothing to try his last hand at preventing the capitulation of the person to Christ.

What can happen, however, is that Christian believers can become *oppressed* by demonic influence. I have no doubt at all that believers are subjected to massive onslaught by Satan and are frequently the subject of attack by denomic forces. Recently I heard of an old missionary to China who always counselled his Christian friends *never* to exorcise by the laying on of hands. He said this because at one time in his own experience he was involved in doing this when he felt the demonic power race up his arm and attempt to invade his own spirit. At that moment he claimed the covering of the blood of Jesus and was saved from hurt, but from that time on he always carried out deliverance ministry without physically touching the subject.

This oppression comes about for a whole number of reasons. It may be the result of the spiritual state of other people around us. Contrary spirits communicate their evil intentions from one person to another very easily. If someone is affected by, say, a spirit of criticism, it will not only be the words of criticism that are communicated but, in the end, the very power of that spirit will communicate itself. Christian communities can become infected by the adverse influence of spiritual evil in this way unless strong and vigilant steps of faith are taken to both prevent it and to stamp it out.

The picture of the Israelites taking the land of Canaan is appropriate here. They entered the land and took possession of it but failed to eradicate every trace of opposition and some enemy-occupied cities were left. Those enclaves were a continual source of trouble to them ever after. If there are areas of weakness or emotional instability or particular vulnerability that we leave undealt with in our lives, then the enemy can take a foothold in these and attempt to gain possession once again. These areas need to be confronted and dealt with in confession and repentance and the victory over demonic oppression claimed in the name of Jesus (Colossians 3.16).

With regard to the life of faith this leads to a number of important factors of which we need to be aware:

Firstly, Jesus made it clear that the intention of Satan is to snatch away the word of faith as soon as it is sown. He speaks of this in the well-known parable of the sower:

'Satan comes and takes away the word that was sown in them' (Mark 4.15).

The Devil knows that faith comes by hearing the word of God. He himself has suffered the effect of that word in his own experience. God's word expelled him from heaven and God's word prevented his attack on Jesus from being successful. His interest in our lives is to snatch away the word of faith.

If for no other reason, this is why we need to examine everything that comes into our lives purporting to be a word of direction during any enterprise of faith. We have learned the need always to go back to the first word that God has spoken and which has been rested in our hearts, minds and lives. Often we have discovered that Satan will stop at nothing to feed in other words which would divert us from the truth that is the ground of faith.

Secondly, the Devil works through a great variety of agencies to seek to achieve his evil design within our lives. Often it takes real revelation from God to recognise that what we are going through finds its roots in the hand of the evil one. We have become too accepting of illness, difficulties, and wrong circumstances as being part of the warp and woof of normal human experience. Without being melodramatic in the wrong way we need to be aware of the many means by which Satan seeks to attack the work of faith in our lives. The Gospels make it very clear that Satan has at his command a whole host of demons whose role is to carry out his purpose of harassment and binding in human lives. The Authorised Version has done us an injustice historically by translating the Greek word '*daimon*' as Devil. The word is demon and the fact is that demons are the local and lesser agents of Satan. They have no independent authority of their own, but only what they derive from the master. That is why when the higher spiritual authority of Jesus is brought to bear upon them they have no power in themselves to resist that. In the words of Charles Wesley:

'Jesus! the name high over all,
In hell, or earth, or sky;
Angels and men before it fall,
And devils fear and fly'.

This is why, in our approach to the work of Satan in our lives we need to bear in mind the exhortation of Paul to the Colossians:

'Whatever you do, whether in word or in deed, do it all in the name of the Lord Jesus' (Colossians 3.17).

But the New Testament makes it just as clear that Satan works through other means. He works through sickness, as in the woman who had been crippled by a spirit for eighteen years (Luke 13.11ff). He can also work through sin:

'He who does what is sinful is of the devil, because the devil has been sinning from the beginning. The reason the Son of God appeared was to destroy the devil's work' (1 John 3.8).

He prevents the word of God having its way within human lives by the power of possessions and the grip they can take on the soul. That is why Jesus expressed just sorrow in his encounter with the rich young ruler (Matthew 19.24).

Whenever we step out in faith we must be aware of the fact that the more alive we are for God the more we stir up activity in the enemy camp.

Thirdly, however, we need always to remind ourselves that Satan is a defeated foe. His power has been severely attenuated by the victory of Calvary and he has no ultimate say in the life of a believer in whom the Holy Spirit dwells. This is what Jesus taught his disciples when they returned from the first mission on their own. They were full of elation because of the effectiveness of their work. Jesus answered:

'I saw Satan fall like lightning from heaven. I have given you authority to trample on snakes and scorpions, and to overcome all the power of the enemy' (Luke 10.18–19).

Satan has been overthrown in the victory of Jesus.

Time and again in the Gospels we are confronted with a head-on clash between the power of Satan and the will of God in the life of Jesus. Never are we left with the impression that Jesus is taken by surprise or that there is the possibility of Satan gaining the upper-hand. His worst deeds, like that of the betrayal of Judas Iscariot, are subsumed under the permissive will of the Father. As in the ancient case of Job, Satan only has his way because it is given him by the Father. In Mark 8 we read of one of Satan's most subtle approaches to Jesus where Peter opposes the suggestion that the Son of Man must suffer. On the surface it seemed to be a good, protective spirit that would save Jesus from an awful fate. At heart it was a cunning device of Satan to try and divert the Son from his mission. Jesus rumbled Satan:

'He rebuked Peter. "Out of my sight, Satan!" he said, "You do not have in mind the things of God, but the things of men"' (Mark 8.33).

We have been provided with everything we need to deal with the attack of evil and the work of the Devil. We need not stand in fear of him. We may stand in respect of him but we don't need to imagine that he has any real authority in our lives.

We have the power of *the blood of Jesus*. Here lies the utlimate secret of the defeat of Satan, because it speaks of the cross and of the work of God in Christ as he confronted the powers of darkness head on. There Satan threw all his fury against the purposes of God but to no avail. In his death and resurrection Jesus has disarmed the powers and authorities and stripped them of any real meaning as far as the believer is concerned.

In his great vision on the island of Patmos, John saw the power of the victory of Jesus:

> 'Now have come the salvation and the power and the kingdom of our God, and the authority of his Christ. For the accuser of our brothers . . . has been hurled down. They overcame him by the blood of the Lamb and by the word of their testimony' (Revelation 12.10).

We have *the indwelling Holy Spirit*. The Holy Spirit lives within us to set us free from any fear of dominion by the powers of evil. His power within us is available to withstand any further attack of demonic and Satanic power:

> 'You, dear children, are from God and have overcome them, because the one who is in you is greater than the one who is in the world' (1 John 4.4).

We have *the full armour of God*. Paul describes the armour of God in the very context of spiritual warfare:

> 'Our struggle is not against flesh and blood, but against the rulers, against the authorities, against the powers of this dark world and against spiritual forces

of evil in the heavenly realms. Therefore put on the full armour of God' (Ephesians 6.12).

Every part of this spiritual armour is fashioned to deal with attacks of the enemy in particular places and by particular methods. We have not been left defenceless against the onslaught of Satan.

We have the encouragement of *the word of God*.

The Scriptures encourage us to withstand the power of Satan knowing that if we do so in the power of God, then there is nothing he can do about it.

'Submit yourselves, then, to God. Resist the devil, and he will flee from you' (James 4.7)

To live by faith we need to have a very clear view of the power of Satan. Like Paul, we need not to be ignorant of his devices but at the same time we need to know that we have the power to overcome him in Christ Jesus.

'In the name of Jesus, In the name of Jesus,
We have the victory.
In the name of Jesus, In the name of Jesus,
Demons will have to flee.
Who can tell what God can do?
Who can tell of his love for you?
In the name of Jesus, Jesus,
We have the victory'.

XVIII

The gift of faith

The story is told about that great man of faith, George Muller of Bristol, of how he was travelling by sea to Canada when the ship became stranded in fog. The captain had been on the bridge continuously as they made their way slowly forward. They were stuck off the coast of Newfoundland and Muller needed to be in Quebec for an important engagement. It was Wednesday and he was meant to be there on the Saturday. From a human point of view the situation seemed hopeless and this was confirmed by the captain when Muller went to speak with him on the bridge. The captain told him that the fog was unrelenting and it would be impossible to make port by Saturday. Muller replied:

'If your boat can't take me, God will find some other way. I've never been late for an appointment in fifty seven years'.

When the captain persisted that there was nothing that could be done, Muller suggested they both went below to pray. 'Mr Muller', the captain said, 'Don't you know how dense the fog is?'

'My eye is not on fog but on God who controls the fog and every circumstance of my life', said Muller.

The two men went to pray but, after Muller had prayed and simply asked God to remove the fog, he stopped the captain from praying because, as he pointed out, there would be little good someone praying who did not believe the prayer would be answered. As soon as Muller had finished praying he invited the captain to open the door and see that the fog had gone. To the captain's astonishment it had, and they were able to continue their journey at full speed and in time for George Muller's appointment.

Muller wrote sometime afterwards in his journal:

'It pleased the Lord to give me in some cases something like the gift of faith; so that unconditionally I could ask and look for an answer'.

George Muller is here putting his finger on something important to the life of faith. I have found this to be the case on more than one occasion, that God provides a special gift of faith for particular needs. He imparts this special gift of faith to enable us to take steps of faith that are beyond the normal level of Christian experience.

We all know that it is essential to have faith even to become a Christian. The experience of new birth depends on faith in Jesus and the power of the Holy Spirit. Not one of us have the human ability to bring ourselves out of our state of estrangement from God into a relationship of love in which our sins are forgiven and our guilt taken away. Ephesians 2.8, makes it clear that faith is the ground of every believer's experience:

'For it is by grace you have been saved, through faith – and this not from yourselves, it is the gift of God – not by works, so that no one can boast'.

It is equally true that faith is the ground of ongoing Christian experience. The Christian believer is called to take his reference, not from the human point of view, but from the insight that faith brings. The words of Paul in 2 Corinthians 5.7, sum up what is true for every Christian:

'We live by faith, not by sight'.

126

So faith is normal and necessary in the life of every Christian. In the words of Hebrews 11.6, 'Without faith it is impossible to please God'.

It is still true, however, that God gives special gifts of faith through the Holy Spirit. This gift is listed among other gifts by Paul in 1 Corinthians 12:

> 'To one there is given through the Spirit the message of wisdom, to another the message of knowledge by means of the same Spirit, to another faith by the same Spirit'.

This gift of faith is given by God to enable us to undertake enterprises of faith or to fulfil special callings which he brings. I have found that this gift ebbs and flows. Even though one might be standing in faith over a period of time, such as the five months we were believing for Roffey Place, the level of faith does not stay the same throughout. There are crises of faith and then there are fallow periods when things seem quieter. The moments of crisis seem to be important as steps forward in the enterprise while during the quieter moments faith relaxes until it is time to take the next urgent step forward.

Muller was right when he said that there is an unconditional aspect to this gift of faith. It seems that the ability is given simply to speak out the faith and know for sure that God will answer. This gift of faith in action is a powerful witness. It is said that every major faith enterprise for years afterwards found its inspiration in the faith of George Muller. That was certainly true in the case of Hudson Taylor, founder of the China Inland Mission, who gained his motivation directly from the testimony of George Muller. Many other orphanages found their inspiration from the same source. Muller himself visited some of these later in his life in places as far apart as Holland and Japan.

This gift of faith, it seems to me, comes with a sense of call or burden. It may not be that this call comes as a blinding flash, it may be that it develops as a sense of obligation. Faith has often been given to Christians who have developed a burden to meet a particular need. Sometimes, as in the case of Roffey Place, the calling comes in an unlikely way at an unexpected time. I cannot say that when I first saw the brochure my heart warmed right away to the idea of being involved in the founding of a college.

As time went, however, and the brochure kept appearing I could not get rid of the thought that this was what God wanted. That thought grew from an embryonic idea to become a powerful sense of call within my spirit until, in the end, I would have had difficulty knowing what else to do if Roffey Place had not materialised.

This special gift of faith has certain characteristics that are important:

It sees. People with the gift of faith see things that other people do not see. They see the vision that God is giving for a particular work or ministry. They see potential where other people see only problems. They see the possibilities and the promises of faith. That is because this gift does not focus on the problem but on the greatness of God. This gift of faith brings vision. It can discern where the hand of God is. It may not know all the details but it can perceive the way ahead and discern which movements are from God and which are not. That is why those with the special gift of faith are in the lead. It is almost as though they are wearing the spiritual radar which can look ahead and avoid the pitfalls.

It knows. This gift of faith operates in conjunction with other spiritual gifts. I find that it is rarely true that the gifts of the Holy Spirit work on their own. It is as though a major gift is given and other gifts come with it to play the minor keys. For example, with the gift of faith is often given the gift of wisdom or the gift of knowledge or one or more of the other spiritual gifts. The reason for this is quite clear. Faith does not stand on its own. Knowledge enlightens faith and wisdom enables faith to understand the ways of God and what steps should be taken. Often a gift of prophecy will be given with faith and I believe that every time a real gift of healing operates it must work through the channel of faith. There is a great interrelationship between the gifts as they operate in our lives.

This is why George Muller was able with such confidence to invite the captain to open the door and see that the fog had gone. That was faith informed by knowledge. The faith enabled him to trust God and the gift of knowledge let him know that his faith had been met.

It acts. Rather it enables us to act. I don't believe that faith is at all a passive affair. There are, of course, moments when we can do nothing but wait, but faith is active. For one thing it is always keeping the pressure up behind the problem. It is this persistency of faith that begins to bring results. Persistence of faith is like a sign of God's persistence in the situation. It is almost like the prophetic symbolism of the Old Testament in which the prophet was asked by God to enact the event he was foretelling before it actually took place. That action of faith on the part of the prophet was a very important element in the main action coming to pass.

I have developed the habit of bringing down a 'faith shutter' in certain circumstances. Imagine, for a moment, a small stream running down a hillside. It has created a small gully and it runs away down into the distance. The water is going somewhere but it has no power in it because the stream is only a trickle. Then imagine that you build a small dam across that stream. Immediately everything changes. The small trickle of water soon collects up behind the dam and a pool is formed. That pool could be used to provide power for a mill-wheel or some other purpose.

It's like that with faith. You can believe for something in a general or continual way but sometimes it is necessary to cause the pressure of faith to build up so that faith and prayer just don't trickle away into the distance. Sometimes when I am standing in faith for a particular purpose, I consciously bring a shutter down in my mind. In faith I look ahead to a specific time of a particular event and see that as the dam across the stream behind which all my praying and believing is going to be caught up. this has the effect from my point of view of bringing a sharp edge to faith. It doesn't mean that the Lord is bound to that but it provides a stop against which faith can be active. I have found that time and again this 'faith shutter' has been a revelation of the Holy Spirit and that the Lord has acted in power by the time set in my mind. The effect is that faith pressure is caused and very often a special breakthrough is achieved by doing this.

I recall, one particular faith act in relation to Roffey Place. To many people it would seem a very unimportant thing, indeed to some it may seem stupid, but there was a hidden power in it, just as there was in the prophetic actions of the prophets which enabled God to move within human experience.

One member of the Fellowship, Francis Pym, with his wife, covenanted to stand with me in a special way on a daily basis. Time and again they shared that faith with me which was a great encouragement in the situation. On one occasion Francis handed me an envelope. At the time we needed about five hundred thousand pounds. Inside the envelope was a five pound note which had been torn in half. As Francis handed me the envelope he indicated that the Lord had told him to undertake this prophetic action as a seed of faith. This was almost a sacramental sign of our prayers. In our hearts was that strong faith for the five hundred thousand pounds. In the event, that small faith action yielded fruit more than one hundred thousand fold!

It grows. The Lord leads us step by step into faith. I can look back over the last few years and see how he had led me step by step from one enterprise to another. At first it was smaller things, now it has grown into huge faith enterprises. It is not, however, the size of the venture of faith that determines the need for faith. George Muller's experience demonstrates how that faith becomes real in situations that for other people may seem trivial and unimportant. They are, however, part of the fabric of life and can prevent or enable the purposes of God.

As we gain experience in faith we gain confidence in

our knowledge of God and of what he will do in any given situation. Faith becomes the language of our lives.

It loves. Paul says in Galations 5.6:

'The only thing that counts is faith expressing itself through love'.

He is underlining an important principle: that the gift of faith, or indeed any of the gifts of the Holy Spirit, cannot be truly effective if they are divorced from the fruit of the spirit in our lives.

'If I have a faith that can move mountains, but have not love, I am nothing' (1 Corinthians 13.2).

This is where the cost of faith comes in, because, if we are to stand in faith for the work of God in the lives of people in great need, then we will need a great anointing of love. Recently I was speaking about this very thing with my colleague David Brown who works to see the deliverance of God in the lives of so many broken and needy men and women. It takes a special anointing of love in the first place to be involved in that ministry and sometimes that love is so painful because of its depth in heart for these people. On the other hand it takes a special anointing of faith continually because so often there is failure or disappointment. Just when it seems things are getting somewhere in the life of a particular individual that person will go and do something completely stupid or rebellious. It is only where faith is mixed with the real love of Jesus that one can continue to minister effectively in that kind of situation.

I sometimes think that faith is like one of those little men who sits on a wall at a funfair sideshow. He sits there to be shot at and is often shot down, but every time he is shot down he pops back. Faith is resilient and if we want to live a life of faith we need to realise that this will be our experience.

It overcomes. Faith is the strongest force in the universe. In fact it is through the gift of faith that God expresses his absolute power. It is his way of overcoming all that is negative and dark and it is the gift he gives his saints to take head on the forces of evil:

'This is the victory that has overcome the world, even our faith' (1 John 5.4).

The gift is available to us through the Holy Spirit. God wants us to discover this gift for our own lives and to experience for ourselves the power of the kingdom of heaven.

XIX

Praying in faith

Praying in faith is sometimes like standing looking at a vast and spectacular range of mountains. It is breathtaking and it strikes you dumb. There is nothing you can say. How can you describe what you are seeing? It is like that with faith. Sometimes when you see the problem you are confronted with and also the greatness of the Lord there is nothing you can do. You just stand there. It is that sense of awe and power and depth and transcendence and greatness that prevents you from saying or doing anything.

Praying in faith is just like that. There are times when you feel it is better to say nothing because to try and say anything would be to risk putting a foot in it. There is a tremendous depth of awe and of waiting before the Lord. When you stand in silence in this kind of prayer it is not because nothing is happening, because, as you stand awe-struck before the mountain, you realise that somebody has done something far more than you could ever do. So you stand there and submit yourself to that something and you are overpowered by it, and the greatness of it takes root in your soul and something happens deep within. You become again the crucible of faith in which the greatness of God and the hugeness of the problem intermix. Of course the sovereignty of God overcomes the problem but it is inside you. You see and feel it taking place. Words cannot express it. It is not just that you don't know what to pray for, or how to pray, it is an overwhelming sense of being overwhelmed as you stand there in the middle of the process.

The Jesus secret

Jesus taught his disciples about faith praying. He said:

> 'When you pray, do not be like the hypocrites, for they
> love to pray standing in the synagogues and on the
> street corners to be seen by men. I tell you the truth,
> they have received their reward in full. When you
> pray, go into your room, close the door and pray to
> your Father, who is unseen. Then your Father, who
> sees what is done in secret, will reward you. And when
> you pray, do not keep on babbling like pagans, for
> they think they will be heard because of their many
> words. Do not be like them, for your Father knows
> what you need before you ask him' (Matthew 6.5–8).

In Jesus' day the Pharisees used to pay a man with a
trumpet to go before them. They would time it to
perfection. The man would stand at a street corner and
blow his trumpet just as the Pharisee appeared to give his
alms. When all the people turned to see what the noise
was about, what they would, in fact, see was the Pharisee
giving his alms to the poor. No wonder Jesus said, 'I tell
you the truth they have received their reward in full'.

My experience is that when your soul is gripped with
the greatness of God and the immensity of the challenge
of faith it has the effect of driving you out of shallowness
into depth. The words of the wise man of Ecclesiastes
express it well:

> 'God is in heaven and you are on earth, so let your
> words be few' (Ecclesiastes 5.2).

Of course this takes up the other significant thought
that Jesus shared with his disciples here. He taught them
they were not to babble like pagans who think they will
be heard because of their many words.

This has been a lesson to me because I have learned
that once you have said something to the Lord you've
said it, and, unless the Lord keeps on telling you to say

it, you may as well relax until he nudges you again. You do get into a sense of urgency in praying in faith when the Spirit makes it urgent. When the Spirit does not make it urgent you cannot work urgency up. It becomes a boredom.

We found this during the five months we were standing in faith for Roffey Place. We had peaks. It was like a mountain range. When it came to a high point, people felt a real sense of urgency. Then there would be two weeks of quiet, then another peak. Sometimes we did not know why the peaks were there. At other times we did know. We knew, for example, that the deposit was due at a certain point and that created a peak of faith. We knew as well when a particular date for completion was due and that created another crisis of faith. At those times there was a great sense of urgency in the Spirit, but there were peaks in between for which we could see no obvious reason. God knew. God knew that there was spiritual warfare going on in the heavenlies. God knew that there were things happening in people's hearts who were unbelievers, perhaps in those from whom we were buying the property, and that those things needed to be dealt with. God knew that there were Christians far away who at that moment were being spoken to in their own spirits about giving money for the project. We didn't know. They were hidden from us but known to the Father. He released the Spirit into our hearts to bring a sense of urgency and we found ourselves gripped with that same sense of faith crisis although we didn't know why. But we got praying and persisted, until the Lord told us in the spirit to stop.

Not long ago a similar thing happened in our morning prayer at Roffey. Everybody was praying together in tongues. There was a great crescendo of noise. I felt the Spirit telling me to stop it and to encourage people to pray simply in English for a while so that we could all say 'Amen', to what they were saying. It meant also that individuals had to understand what they were saying and have the courage to speak openly amongst the congregation. This is a far greater challenge than everyone speaking in tongues at once. Of course it is essential to have corporate tongues, particularly in the realm of spiritual warfare when Christians stand together in the power of Christ against the forces of spiritual evil, but sometimes it can be a cop-out. It can be a cover that permits people to escape the responsibility and challenge of speaking out simply in faith.

Intercession

We often use the word *intercession* to describe faith praying without really knowing what we mean. Is intercession a particularly strong or intense way of praying? Is it particularly associated with spiritual warfare? Does it fulfil a special function relative to other ways of praying?

It may come as a surprise to some that the Greek word commonly translated *intercession* or *to intercede* only occurs some five or six times in the New Testament. In most of these cases it is not speaking of a human activity at all but of something that belongs to the sphere of divine interest.

Take, for example, Romans 8.26–39. The idea of intercession occurs twice in this passage. First, in verses 26 and 27, with reference to the work of the Holy Spirit in the heart of the believer:

'In the same way, the Spirit helps us in our weakness. We do not know what we ought to pray, but the Spirit himself intercedes for us with groans that words cannot express. And he who searches our hearts knows the mind of the Spirit, because the Spirit intercedes for the saints in accordance with God's will.'

I believe that here we are at the heart of what faith prayer really is. Faith praying is not what I do but rather what God does in me by the Holy Spirit. We become channels or vessels in which God himself acts. It isn't a matter of me saying prayers. Sometimes there is nothing at all that I can do, but I allow my spirit to be open to the Father so that he can send the Spirit who begins a divine activity of urgency and intercession in me. It is not my intercession, it is God interceding in me. That is the secret of faith praying. That is why the New Testament speaks of God's movement rather than ours.

In Romans 8.34 the thought of intercession moves from earth to heaven:

> 'Christ Jesus, who died – more than that, who was raised to life – is at the right hand of God and is also interceding for us'.

We may describe this as the divine connection. The Holy Spirit intercedes in me, Jesus intercedes for me. The very same thought regarding the intercessory work of Christ is presented in Hebrews 7.24–25:

> 'Because Jesus lives forever, he has a permanent priesthood. Therefore he is able to save completely those who come to God through him, because he always lives to intercede for them'.

The reality of this intercessory work of Christ for us is the very ground of faith:

> 'Therefore, since we have a great high priest who has gone through the heavens, Jesus the Son of God, let us hold firmly to the faith we profess. For we do not have a high priest who is unable to sympathize with our weaknesses but we have one who has been tempted in every way, just as we are – yet was without sin. Let us then approach the throne of grace with confidence, so that we may receive mercy and find grace to help us in our time of need' (Hebrews 4.14–16).

The only clear instance, in my view, of intercession being described from the human side in the New Testament arises in 1 Timothy 2.1 where the word appears in a list of different kinds of prayer:

'I urge then, first of all, that requests, prayers, inter-cession and thanksgiving be made for everyone – for kings and all those in authority, that we may live peaceful and quiet lives in all godliness and holiness'.

This makes the very point that intercession is of a different nature from other praying. It requires a real openness of spirit so as to allow God to work within us his burden and his faith in the power of the Holy Spirit.

If we take the idea of intercession further we can see how important it is to the life of faith, because at the heart of intercession is the idea of *standing between*.

The word that the Authorised Version uses to describe this is *daysman*, that is a person who stood between two opposing parties to bring reconciliation between them. In his reply to Bildad the Shuhite, Job replies with anguish:

'If only there were someone to arbitrate between us, to lay his hand upon us both' (Job 9.33)

This is the very idea that is present in 1 Timothy 2.5 in relation to the work of Christ:

'For there is one God and one mediator between God and men, the man Christ Jesus, *who gave himself as a ransom for all men*'.

This Scripture takes us even deeper into the idea of the *daysman*. The Greek word for mediator is *mesites*. It not only meant that the mediator stood between two oppos-ing factions but that he had to bring peace between them *even if it meant great cost to himself*. It may be that he himself would have to bear the price of paying off a bad debt that was owed, so that peace could be restored between the parties involved. That, of course, is exactly how the New Testament presents us with the idea of Jesus as our mediator. He bore the cost of our sin in his own body on the tree. Without that there would have been no possibility of reconciliation between ourselves and the Father.

It also highlights for us the depth of intercession as a means of faith.

Moses is perhaps the greatest Old Testament example of a *go-between*. Many times he stood between the people and God when they sinned and when God threatened to bring the covenant relationship to an end. Take, for example, Exodus 32.32, where Moses takes upon himself the whole responsibility of an intercessor:

> 'But now, please forgive their sin – but if not, then blot me out of the book you have written'.

Paul felt that same anguish on behalf of his fellow Jews who were rejecting Christ:

> 'For I could wish that I myself were cursed and cut off from Christ for the sake of my brothers, those of my own race, the people of Israel' (Romans 9.3).

And this was from the man whose chief end in life was to see Christ and share in the power of his resurrection! Yet such was the depth of the Spirit's intercession in his soul that he was willing to pay the ultimate cost for the sake of the salvation of every other Jew.

Intercession is not a word that we should use lightly. It expresses the heart of God and it carries with it the burden of paying the price for our prayers to be answered. We're back to the idea of a crucible. If faith is going to work it needs to work in us. We need to bear the burden, be willing to pay the price, stand in that lonely place between heaven and earth and allow the victory of faith to be achieved in us so that it can be released into the situation for which we are praying.

The language of faith

A whole number of different words are used in the New Testament to speak about prayer, but they express four important ideas.

Expressing longing. There is a very proper sense in which

the idea of desire or longing stands at the heart of faith prayer. In Matthew 6 the same word is used of the hypocrites as of the disciples. It is a word that expresses longing or desire. At heart, prayer is getting what we long for. The trouble with the Pharisees is that they only longed for what they wanted for themselves. That is why Jesus said: 'They have received their reward in full'.

Faith praying is not about me fulfilling my selfish desires but about my desiring the will of God. It is where my desires have been overtaken by God's will and my longing is now what the Father wants and I long to see the Father working in mighty power and bringing his purpose to pass.

When Roffey Place first came on to the market I really didn't want to know deep down inside. God had to create that longing inside my heart so that I could share his desire for the place. After about three weeks, and as the vision took shape in my heart, I developed a real desire to go to Roffey Place. I stood on top of the sewage plant there one day and I prayed, 'Lord, give me this place'. And so God's will became my will and we prayed with desire.

I don't believe you get anywhere praying for what you don't want.

Asking Father. The real thing about praying in faith is that you know what you have asked for. I sometimes think we don't get the answers because we're not quite sure what the question was. Jesus himself urged us to ask so that it would be given to us:

'Ask and it will be given to you; seek and you will find; knock and the door will be opened to you. For everyone who asks receives; he who seeks finds; and to him who knocks, the door will be opened' (Matthew 7.7–8).

The idea of asking in prayer runs right through the New Testament. That is because the most powerful relationship of faith is that which stands between Father and son. In Christ Jesus we have become sons and daughters of God. The Father stands with his arms stretched out waiting to give us the blessings of faith. What we need to do is come and ask him:

> 'Dear friends, if our hearts do not condemn us, we have confidence before God and receive from him anything we ask, because we obey his commands and do what pleases him' (1 John 3, 21–22).

Jesus said:

> 'You may ask me for anything in my name, and I will do it' (John 14.14).

I am reminded of the apocryphal story of the old Yorkshire Methodist who went to the weeknight prayer meeting. During the meeting a rather eloquent brother launched forth in prayer. He continued for a very long time and he finished with a triumphant flourish, 'And now, O Lord, what more can man say unto thee?' The old Yorkshireman pulled his coat-tails and advised him: 'Ask him for summat and shut up!'

Feeling urgent. Can you imagine how old Zechariah felt in his prayers? Luke 1.7 tells us that he and his wife Elizabeth had no children,

> 'because Elizabeth was barren; and they were both well on in years'.

I guarantee there was a note of urgency about Zechariah's praying. At least that is what the word that is used to describe his prayer implies. He had besought the Lord for a long time. Imagine his joy when the angel announced to him that his cry had been heard:

> 'Do not be afraid, Zechariah; your prayer has been heard. Your wife Elizabeth will bear you a son' (Luke 1.13).

The old idea is of *supplication*, of a special pleading and hanging on to something. There is a tenacity about this urgency. At heart it knows it's right and it won't let go until it sees the proper outcome. The same word is used in James 5.16:

'Therefore confess your sins to each other and pray for each other so that you may be healed. The *prayer* of a righteous man is powerful and effective'.

Actually, the Authorized Version maintains the note of urgency much better than the New International Version. It says:

'The effectual fervent prayer of a righteous man availeth much'.

In the case of Zechariah it seems that he had been praying in earnest for a long time for his wife Elizabeth to have a baby. Now that he was growing old and his wife was getting beyond the point of child-bearing, that earnestness took on an increased sense of urgency. The idea of beseeching God like this almost has a timetable built into it. It was God's time to give Zechariah the answer to his prayer because it fitted in perfectly with his plan for Jesus. The urgency of Zechariah built up in relation to that so the timetable of God was fulfilled in perfection.

I know just what that means. It is almost as though two movements are taking place at once. There is the movement of urgency in your own heart and there is the movement of God's will in the situation. The fulfilment of that will comes from one direction and the sense of urgency from another, like two roads that are heading for an intersection. Suddenly they cross each other. When you pray in faith that is just what happens. You can almost feel yourself moving along in the Spirit towards an appointed time. You can feel the Holy Spirit pulling you along a road and you sense there is going to be a meeting with God. You sense that you are going to run into the will of God, and you do.

Standing firm. One of the New Testament words for prayer, *proseuche* in particular carries with it the idea of persisting or of pouring out in prayer. It is a word that occurs many, many times in the New Testament. In the experience of Jesus we discover how he stood firm in prayer:

'One of those days Jesus went out into the hills to pray, and spent the night praying to God'. (Luke 6.12).

It's the same word that is used in Matthew 21.22:

'If you believe, you will receive whatever you ask for in prayer'.

I believe this is one reason why our prayer agenda is often so long and diffuse. We get easily bored about standing in faith over one particular issue. Yet persistence is one of the hallmarks of real faith praying. It is significant that on the occasion when Jesus came back down the mountain and found his disciples struggling to free the boy with an evil spirit, it is this word that is used. In his response to the disciples Jesus said:

'This kind can come out only by prayer'.

Involved in that situation was a large element of struggle and the only kind of praying that will overcome is that persistent, strong prayer of faith. Some versions add the words *and fasting*.

Now if you add fasting to prayer what you get is a movement in which you are persisting before the Lord. As long as you fast you pray. That is one of the important facts about fasting. Fasting of itself is neither here nor there, but the whole idea is associated with other actions. If I fast for a day it not only takes my mind off other things and makes time for God, it creates a boundary for prayer. It is really the context within which prayer is going to work. Fasting makes me God-conscious and it gives me time to become prayer-active.

All these ideas express different dimensions of faith prayer. They are like the step ladders of faith.

XX

Footprints of faith

I have found that this exercise of faith through prayer develops step by step. As I look back I can almost see the footprints in the sand that have brought me to this place. Each step logically leads to the next.

Waiting on God

'Be still and know that I am God,' says the Psalmist and that is absolutely true. As we begin to wait before the Lord the Holy Spirit begins to move deeply within our hearts.

Conviction

The first movement that takes place in our spirits is that of conviction:

> 'Who may ascend the hill of the Lord?
> Who may stand in his holy place?
> He who has clean hands and a pure heart,
> who does not lift up his soul to an idol
> or swear by what is false' (Psalm 24. 3–4).

How do we get from where we are to being able to move on to the hill of the Lord? It is by the convicting power of the Holy Spirit. John, in his letter, speaks of the power of faith within a heart that is clean before the Lord:

> 'Dear friends, if our hearts do not condemn us, we
> have confidence before God and receive from him
> anything we ask, because we obey his commands and
> do what pleases him' (1 John 3.21–22).

John is speaking about the clarity that comes to our spirits as the Holy Spirit shows us our sin before the Father, enables us to turn away from our sin in repentance, and brings forgiveness in the blood of Jesus.

'If we confess our sins, he is faithful and just and will forgive us our sins and purify us from all unrighteousness' (1 John 1.9).

Waiting on God brings about a confidence in God because it clears our hearts from condemnation. Faith needs confidence – not self-confidence, but God-confidence and that comes when our old selves are put out of the way and God cleanses our lives.

The Devil believes in conviction as well. He doesn't mind at all if we feel bad about our sins. What he wants to prevent in our hearts is that godly movement from conviction through confession into cleansing. We need to become experienced in that process of cleansing because that is what brings power to faith. The Devil wants to make sure that conviction is a dead-end. His purpose is that it will take a nose-dive and end up in guilt rather than in the full freedom of forgiveness. But when we go through conviction to confession, we end up being cleansed. It is an upward movement as far as God is concerned and it prepares the heart for faith as we wait before him in prayer.

Thanksgiving

The instruction of Paul in Philippians 4.6 is more than decent theology at this point. Paul enjoins his readers to come in their prayers with thanksgiving:

'Do not be anxious about anything, but in everything, by prayer and petition, with thanksgiving, present your requests to God'.

We need to develop good memories as far as faith is concerned, to be able to bring to mind all the good things that God has already done. This provides encouragement and stimulus for new ventures of faith to which we are called. This is why in the experience of the Israelites, the Lord provided them with the means to exercise their faith memories. Whenever God did something outstanding for them he instructed them in ways of remembering. Sometimes they were given special words to repeat, at other times they marked the site of God's miracle in their lives.

Samuel did that. When the Lord gave him a great victory over the Philistines, he built a stone pillar and called it *Ebenezer* (a pillar of help). Joshua was told to do the same sort of thing on the day that the Lord led the people through the waters of the Jordan in full flood to enter the Promised Land:

'Each of you is to take up a stone on his shoulder,
according to the number of the tribes of the Israelites,
to serve as a sign among you. In the future, when your
children ask you, "What do these stones mean?" tell
them that the flow of the Jordan was cut off before the
ark of the covenant of the Lord' (Joshua 4.5–7).

These were visual aids to the memory of faith. As long as they saw these signs they could never doubt that God was able to deliver them. So it is with us. We need to allow the Holy Spirit to develop a spirit of thanksgiving by bringing to mind our recollections of faith. He goes into the back of our minds, into those old dusty files that have been forgotten for years, and he brings them out and opens them again to our imagination. He vivifies the memories of faith and makes us relive the good things of God. Like the Psalmist, we begin to praise the Lord:

'Praise the Lord, O my soul;
all my inmost being, praise his holy name.
Praise the Lord, O my soul,
and forget not all his benefits' (Psalm 103.1–2).

Praise is the foundation on which faith is built. Faith cannot operate out of doubt, faith cannot operate out of unthankfulness, faith cannot operate out of a depressed spirit. Faith operates hand in hand with thanksgiving which lifts our eyes away from ourselves and enables us to see God in his true greatness.

Revelation

It is revelation that provides the motivation when we pray in faith. The work of the Holy Spirit within our hearts is to bring us to a place of understanding the will of God. We come to know what it is that we should be praying about and how we should be praying.

In my last book, HOW MUCH MORE, I told the remarkable story of how my wife Hilda once had a tremendous burden placed on her heart for a little girl called Annabel Schild who had been kidnapped by Sardinian terrorists. How do you pray in that kind of situation? She had only heard about it, like everyone else, through television news and was only one of millions of Christians. Yet she woke up one morning with a tremendous burden from God that she should spend her time praying for this particular girl. Nobody knew whether she was alive or dead, but God showed Hilda how to pray. For three hours she prayed in tongues until God broke through and gave her a vision of the little girl sitting in a cave in the mountains alive and well. She then knew that what she had to pray for was the girl's release. Nobody else knew the girl was alive, but God revealed that directly to Hilda by the Holy Spirit. It was worth praying for her release. And so for four days she prayed until on the Saturday morning of that week she woke up, turned on the radio, and heard to her own joy and amazement that the girl had been found safe wandering on a mountain road after having been set free by her captives.

You see, that is what happens when we wait before the Lord. He will take something out of his store of problems and place it on our heart. We will become his crucible of faith. Sometimes it will be something immediate to our own experience, as Roffey Place was for us, at other times it will be a burden for someone way beyond the bounds of our own experience that we know nothing directly about.

Revelation stands at the heart of faith because through it we can share in the thoughts and purposes of the Father as he brings them to pass in his power.

Exercising the Spirit

The Spirit is a part of our inner being that tends to suffer from neglect.

How do we exercise the spirit as we stand in faith? Well fortunately we have been given some good apparatus with which to train. We need to open ourselves up to the movement of the Holy Spirit. This is where the gift of tongues comes into its own. If you don't know what to pray for or how to proceed then it is a very good exercise for the spirit to allow the Holy Spirit to lead you in the exercise of tongues. Tongues don't come just as a glossolalia, a jabbering, they are actually a movement of the spirit and those who learn to speak in tongues properly are not necessarily those who jabber away incessantly. A real fight of tongues starts deep down and it is an exercise of the spirit before the Father. Through tongues we begin to search our own spirit and allow it to flex its muscles.

Another means of spiritual exercise is by using Scripture. As you wait quietly before the Scripture it begins to have that opening-out effect in your own spirit. It is almost like the effect of a shower of rain breaking up ground that has become dry and dusty. That is how the power of the word of God is described in Isaiah 55.10:

'As the rain and snow come down from heaven,
and do not return to it
without watering the earth. . . .
so is my word that goes out from my mouth:
It will not return to me empty,
but will accomplish what I desire
and achieve the purpose for which I sent it'.

Another very good thing for exercising the spirit is the gift of praise. Praise has a magnetic quality about it. You can start praising the Lord with your tongue and your voice but gradually it attracts the spirit. If your spirit is dormant and you start to praise the Lord it will attract your spirit to life. There is an obedience in praise. It has not just got to do with our feelings and emotions. Praise is obedience because it has this magnetic quality about it. God has given us the gift of praise to raise our spirits out of their slumber and to make them aware of his greatness.

It is the same with worship. There is a difference between praise and worship. Praise is a stand-up, extrovert thing: worship is a deep introvert thing which adores, worships and loves the Father. It is the sweet whispers of love through the Spirit into the ear of God.

These are the dumb-bells of the spirit, the fitness machines that God has given us to exercise our inner being. They make us fit for faith.

Seeing the way

As far as the Scriptures are concerned, faith and love have at least one important feature in common. They are not blind. The love of God is not blind. It does not cover up our sins, it covers *over* them. But not before it has looked them full in the face and dealt with them in the power of Calvary.

Neither is faith blind. It knows where it is going. A common secular view of faith looks upon it as a 'leap in the dark'. To the modern existentialist this kind of faith is the only alternative to suicide in a world of meaninglessness, but it is completely the opposite of biblical faith. Biblical faith does not walk in the dark. According to Hebrews 11.1:

'Faith is being sure of what we hope for and certain of what we do not see'.

It is not seen perhaps by the human eye, but it is visible to faith. As you begin to flex your spirit, God will begin to show you things. He will do it through the gifts of the Holy Spirit. He will do it by means of dreams and visions. He will do it through the witness of Scripture. He will do it through the guidance and words of fellow believers. He will show you things that other people around you do not see. This is the difference between living in hopefulness and praying in faith. Faith prayer has a certainty and assurance that comes from God.

Sometimes I think that faith is like a picture where you start with the frame and then do the filling in instead of a jigsaw where you start with the small piece and gradually build it into a meaningful whole. Faith sees the framework and God takes the pen in your hand and does the filling in. Faith sees the vision, it feels the perimeters of the vision, it knows the boundaries, but it might not know the details.

Man apart from faith is bothered about all the details: Can we complete by this date? What house shall I live in? Exactly how much money shall I earn in a year? Could you please tell me the precise programme of events? Faith does not worry about such things at the outset. They will be filled in as God moves. That was the choice which Jesus presented to his followers. Faith is a philosophy of life that is diametrically opposed to secular thinking.

'Seek first his kingdom and his righteousness, and all these things will be given to you as well' (Matthew 6.33).

Gaining assurance

Of course the whole of Christian life is based on assurance. It begins with the assurance that comes from the Holy Spirit that we are born of God.

'The Spirit himself testifies with our spirit that we are God's children' (Romans 8.16).

150

Apart from that basic certainty we cannot take our first step of faith. Nobody else can tell us this; it is an assurance that comes from the Father himself. Faith moves on in assurance. It comes from waiting on God and hearing the whisper of the Holy Spirit in our heart. It comes through the promises of Scripture that confirm and help us to understand what we are hearing inside. Faith and assurance go hand in hand together.

It is this gift of assurance through the Holy Spirit that enables us to take the next step of faith. It was exactly this that Colin Urquhart received in that hotel bedroom in Singapore when God first confirmed to his own spirit that the rest of the money for Roffey Place was secure. The effect of this was to transform what had been tentative agreement and action into faith certainty. From that moment on he acted and spoke as though the money was already in his pocket. In fact it was as good as there. It was this certainty of faith that the ancient saints were commended for according to Hebrews 11:

> 'By faith Abraham, when called to go to a place he would later receive as his inheritance, obeyed and went, even though he did not know where he was going. . . . For he was looking forward to the city with foundations, whose architect and builder is God' (Hebrews 11.8–10).

You see Abraham worked with that framework of faith and allowed God to paint in the details as he went. What kept him following in faith was the inner certainty of spirit that he had received through his personal meeting with God.

Claiming the victory

The dramatic vision of Daniel 10 provides for us an insight into the hidden realms of faith. Daniel had been asking for God's help for some time and it seemed to be slow in arriving. The man who appeared to him in a vision explained the reason:

'Since the first day that you set your mind to gain understanding and to humble yourself before your God, your words were heard, and I have come in response to them. But the prince of the Persian kingdom resisted me twenty-one days. Then Michael, one of the chief princes, came to help me, because I was detained there'. (Daniel 10.12–13).

Faith operates in the context of spiritual warfare and a real element of faith praying is taken up with the need to engage in that battle. Satan's purpose is to try and prevent the word of God being fulfilled. But the Father has given us some strong medicine with which to destroy the works of Satan:

'The one who is in you is greater than the one who is in the world' (1 John 4.4).

Faith stands on its feet and claims the victory of Jesus. I have spoken elsewhere already about the power of the word of God and of the significance of the finished work of Jesus on the Cross with regard to the victory of faith. To claim the victory, faith fixes on these accomplished works of God.

It is very important if we are to achieve victory that we don't go by outward circumstances. That is exactly what the Devil would like us to do. Often in the life of faith things seem to get worse before they get better. I remember the feeling I experienced after the second date had passed for completion of the deal. It was bad enough after the first a month before, but now it felt as though all was lost. In the intervening month not a thing had happened. We were no nearer getting the remaining money that was needed than before. There was no earthly reason why it should be any different before the next and absolutely final date for completion arrived, but that is the very time to claim the victory of faith.

The victory of faith is claimed on the strength of what God has said or done. What we had to do was go right back to the first promises that God had given us which I have spoken about in the early part of this book. These had to come to life in our spirits once again and they did. As we listened again to the words that God had given us they were quickened inside us and we tackled the situation and the onslaught of the enemy with new vigour and revived faith.

The strategy of Satan has never changed. He always tries to cast doubt on the word of God. The way to oppose him has not changed either. Jesus himself taught us that lesson as he stood against the Devil in the power of God's word. We will only ever know a real victory in faith if what we are standing in is the word of God. With that word we need have no fear:

'This is the victory that has overcome the world, even our faith. Who is it that overcomes the world? Only he who believes that Jesus is the Son of God' (1 John 5.4–5).

XXI

Out of the melting pot

In a minor way it must have been something like what the Jews felt as they walked the streets of Jerusalem when they came back from exile. Most of those Jews had never seen the Holy city. They had probably heard about it from their parents and elders who had been taken away from it seventy years before by the Babylonians. Now, under a new and more beneficient Persian rule, they were allowed to go back and repossess their old homeland.

They entered the city in amazement:

'When the LORD brought back the captives to Zion,
we were like men who dreamed.
Our mouths were filled with laughter,
our tongues with songs of joy.
Then it was said among the nations,
"The Lord has done great things for them".
The Lord has done great things for us,
and we are filled with joy.
. . .

He who goes out weeping,
carrying seed to sow,
will return with songs of joy,
carrying sheaves with him' (Psalm 126.1–3, 6).

On the Tuesday morning after I had heard from Colin about the final provision of three hundred thousand pounds to purchase Roffey Place, I had the privilege of standing up in front of the whole Fellowship at our morning communion and giving them the news. For a few minutes there was a stunned silence. The sense of

God's greatness pervaded the place. We all knew in that moment that touch of amazement that is the gift of faith. Faith never ceases to be surprised. It knows that the Father can do all things. He is able

'to do immeasurably more than all we ask or imagine' (Ephesians 3.20).

Nevertheless, every time God breaks through in power and faith sees its answer, there is that sense of wonder. In the meeting that morning there was almost complete silence for a moment as the immensity of what God had done broke through into people's hearts. This sense of wonder is a tremendous bonus of faith.

The same thing happened the following Monday morning in my own home. That morning we were able to confirm what the Lord had done with the completion of the contract. I had already met with the officials of the RSPCA on the Friday when the money was secure, but the very last step was taken after the weekend. We sat there in silence with that sense of washed-outness that comes from amazement. Only six days before it had seemed impossible. Everybody knew that we were three hundred thousand pounds short. Even the local paper had run a report which, while it was sympathetic, made the situation very clear. The RSPCA had indicated that this was the last chance to complete and no doubt wondered how on earth we would ever achieve it.

Well the real answer is that it was achieved in heaven. Every time God moves like this through faith, whether in a large or small way, there is always this sense of wonder. God has acted in a way for all to see. It is unmistakable and undeniable. It is a miracle of faith.

It is important that we never lose this sense of wonder. This is what keeps us from taking things for granted. It is what brings intrinsic value to the gifts of God. When you get something for nothing there is always the danger that you will fail to appreciate its real value and lose the sense of worthwhileness there ought to be. But when God moves heaven and earth to bring something about through faith, it is nothing like that.

I gathered my household together and we all got into the car and went to see Roffey Place through new eyes. What a difference! As we walked round the house and the college, there was a tremendous sense of what God had done. No longer was it a place that belonged to other people, for which we were standing in faith. It was the house of the Lord! It didn't matter to me at that moment what it had been used for before; I knew that God was going to do great things in this place through the lives of men and women whom he would touch here. We sang the song from the words of Jeremiah the prophet:

'Ah, Lord God, thou hast made the heavens
and the earth by they great power.
Ah, Lord God, thou hast made the heavens
and the earth by thine outstretched arm.
Nothing is too difficult for thee.
Nothing is too difficult for thee.
O great and mighty God,
Great in council, mighty in deed,
Nothing, nothing, absolutely nothing,
Nothing is too difficult for thee.'

Two weeks later we moved into the large house that adjoins the college. As the furniture van swung off the main road under the low arching trees that bridge the front drive, I had that tremendous feeling that we were entering into the inheritance of the Lord. It had a strange effect. Instead of feeling greatly elated or carried away with the joy of the situation at that moment, I felt a great sense of humility. Jesus said:

'If you have faith as small as a mustard seed, you can say to this mountain, "Move from here to there" and it will move' (Matthew 17.20).

We had planted seed all right. It is at moments like this you begin to realise how small those seeds seem to be. I have come to see that faith breeds humility of spirit. Faith does not boost our ego. It is a great privilege to be right in the centre of a tremendous move of God, but it has the effect of letting you understand that it is God and not yourself who is at work.

We were not the first folks to come and live at Roffey Place. Just after we had placed the deposit, the resident caretaker had moved out of his house and the RSPCA asked if we wanted someone to go and live there to keep an eye on it against vandalism or intruders. I asked Dick and Paula Worth to go and stay in the caretaker's house until we had completed the deal. That was a seed of faith.

At the time, I remember saying to Dick and Paula that their being there was like a sign from the Lord. I felt that once we had established a foothold, we would not go back on it. It was a bit like the spies entering the land on behalf of the children of Israel; the only thing was that the people were all going to follow right away instead of spending forty years in the wilderness. That was a costly move for the Worths because for those four months they were very much by themselves in the college with only occasional visits from myself or other members of the Fellowship. But it was important and I am sure their continued presence was one of the factors God used to show the RSPCA we really were in earnest about the eventual purchase of the college.

I know that when we arrived it was like being received by those who had gone before to spy out the land. Another important factor was that their presence established for us an important outpost for prayer right in the heart of the territory that God wanted to possess. I am sure, as I look back, that they were the only couple who could have fulfilled that role in the way they did. In practical terms it meant that by the time we got possession of the place, Dick was so familiar with all the plant that we could get moving very quickly indeed establishing the new Christian Training Centre. The miracle was that only two and half months after moving in, we were able to open the doors to an almost full complement of students. It seemed that the Lord had not only provided the funds to buy the place, and the people to get it started, but he had the first batch of students on the sidelines just waiting to come as soon as we were ready. In fact, it was this that God really used to keep my faith alive at times through the months of waiting. Every now and again I would receive a letter from someone I had never heard of, asking if we had a training college or some place where they could come to study and experience the deeper ways of the Holy Spirit. By the time we opened the doors for the first term, we had received more approaches than we could handle in the first instance.

The image that Jesus uses of the kingdom of heaven being like a mustard seed is one that lives very powerfully in my experience:

> 'The kingdom of heaven is like a mustard seed, which a man took and planted in his field. Though it is the smallest of all your seeds, yet when it grows, it is the largest of garden plants and becomes a tree, so that the birds of the air come and perch in its branches' (Matthew 13.31, 32).

God's seeds grow big! Faith looks so small to the outsider. It seems a most foolish way of acting and living, but faith focuses on the power of God. As Paul says:

> 'The foolishness of God is wiser than man's wisdom, and the weakness of God is stronger than man's strength' (1 Corinthians 1.25)

We're only at the beginning. This seed of faith is going to be part of a large tree. Its branches will reach out for the healing of men. God never gives us faith only for ourselves. Faith lets the kingdom grow. Faith is like a pebble that has been dropped in the middle of a pond. The ripples extend wider and wider until they seem to cover the whole pond. Faith is the most evangelistic power in the whole world. It is magnetic because it lets men see the power of God at work today.

We prepared the rooms, cleaned the kitchens, set up the offices and settled in. We consecrated the whole enterprise to God in faith, and finally, on the fence outside, we put the sign, ROFFEY PLACE CHRIST-IAN TRAINING CENTRE.

It was the end – of the beginning!